Conversations with Jesus

How an Alcoholic and Anorexic Found Deep Joy in Christ

Foreword

Mike Phillips often said, "The church is full of suffering people." He knew this well. He was one of those people.

Mike suffered from alcoholism from his teenage years in the late 1970s until he quit drinking in 1994. His tremendous struggle helped him develop into an outstanding drug and alcohol abuse counselor who understood his clients and sympathized deeply with them. When Mike's health failed and he had to quit work, he attended as many AA meetings as he could just to be there for others who had suffered and struggled as he did.

Mike also suffered immensely as an anorexic. This illness led his weight to drop from about 150 pounds in high school to 100 in his thirties, and even lower by the time of his death, at age 48, in 2010. But even as anorexia tormented him, Mike lived a life of inspiring charity. The *Catholic Sun* published an article titled "His Life is a Lesson," and described how on a social worker's salary, Mike donated some $250,000 to Catholic Relief Services.

His illness also led him to a deep personal relationship with Jesus, as in so many ways he entered into an understanding of the mystical suffering of Christ. This relationship and Mike's understanding of suffering appear profoundly in his journal in the pages that follow. When Mike's conversations with Jesus began, around the time he quit drinking, his anorexia was already very severe. Some psychologists would classify it as a personality disorder: being an anorexic, and suffering all the torments that came with it, was simply who Mike was. Short of a miracle, there was no cure, and that miracle never came, but Mike faced his illness with great courage and found great consolation and joy in Christ.

We publish his conversations with Jesus for everyone who is suffering. Not every illness can be overcome, and death is inevitable for us all. But we hope that during their sufferings, some people can find greater joy in Christ through Mike's writings.

All the proceeds from this book will be used to benefit Catholic Relief Services and assist hungry people around the world.

Introduction

Suffering is too big a mystery for me to explain, but I can share my experiences. Suffering is a teacher. If I let it, it can cleanse and purify me to see that only love gives meaning to life, only love transcends pain, and only love endures. Pain can make me either more loving or more hateful—it's my choice.

Evil and suffering do exist. God created us in His image, and we have free will: we can chose to love or to hate. Love brings about healing and happiness, and hate brings about evil and suffering. But because we're all connected, any evil affects all of us, and nature too. It's like dropping a single pebble in a pond. The ripples spread across the whole. In the same way, love brings healing and happiness to all of us.

God is always with us. He does not want us to suffer. He sent His Son, Jesus, to show us how to live, to suffer, to love, and to overcome the evil that results from our poor choices. Jesus was crucified and experienced our brokenness and abandonment. He too was an innocent victim, but he never stopped giving, forgiving, and loving. His love overpowered hate, evil, sin, and suffering, and He is present with us in our own suffering to show us the mystery of life and suffering and to let us taste God's love and save us from our brokenness.

Many people suffer horrendously even though they are innocent. I can't claim to have suffered as intensely as many people have, but again, I can share my experiences. Some bad things happened to me as a child. At times, my life was a nightmare and I felt like garbage. As I grew up, I sought relief in alcohol, and in the long run it made the nightmare worse. And when, one day, I was too sick to go on, I broke down, devastated, and my heart became open to God and His healing love.

It wasn't until I was in my 20s that I was able to talk about my experiences. I was blessed to have a loving family and a priest to listen and support me. I'm wounded and scarred now, but it's ok. I have found that suffering helps me let go of my unhealthy attachments and open myself to what is perfect and meaningful: God, His love, and the love of others, especially when that love isn't easy. My suffering and that of others breaks my heart open to let me meet my God. Only through His grace am I not destroyed by evil, and I am thankful for the hard times that have led me to be more loving and loved. In my brokenness, God can fill me with Himself. I'm truly happy and blessed by Him. May He bless us all.

Who was Michael Phillips?

My son, Michael Phillips, died at the age of 48 from complications of the eating disorder anorexia. I believe that he gave me a sign from the other side of the grave to tell his story.

Michael's life had three major parts. He was deeply spiritual. He was extremely generous. And he was very loving.

Michael would spend between an hour and an hour and a half in silent prayer every morning, using the Jesus prayer. His day was centered on celebrating the Eucharist and receiving the true presence of Jesus. His prayerful reflection was centered on the Passion of Jesus, and Lent was his favorite time of the year.

He died on the universal feast of Paul of the Cross, the mystic who founded the Passionate Congregation. Passionist priests wear a cross over the heart of Jesus on the front of their clerical clothes. Michael wore a large cross on the back of his own clothing, which brought him both ridicule and encouragement.

Michael gave away all his money. His favorite charity was Catholic Relief Services (CRS). After taking care of food, shelter, and clothing for his own very meager lifestyle, he donated whatever was left to CRS. The only exception was when he wanted to help out some particular person in need. When his health forced him to retire, Michael wrote to CRS to tell them he would no longer be able to contribute because he would have just enough money to live on. They wrote back to tell Michael that he was the longest large-gift giver in their history. He probably gave them more than a quarter million dollars, all told, on a salary in the mid-thirty thousands. When he was working, he basically had no savings or checkbook balance.

Michael worked as a certified drug and alcohol counselor. His clients included people mandated by the justice system to receive counseling and people held in our local jail. Michael never revealed specifics about his clients to protect their confidence, but he would often comment that it was a privilege to know a particular person. He also said that everyone had a story, and that there was goodness in every person. The priest who served as the jail chaplain told me once that when Michael walked into a prison pod—all ninety pounds of him—all the inmates would get excited and try to talk to him. Michael touched many lives as a counselor, and people would stop him just to thank him when he was out for a walk.

Michael is buried in a cemetery on Main Street in his hometown of Binghamton. His family stops by often to pay their respects. As the second anniversary of his death approached, I still had many writings of his writings in my possession, although I had never looked through those in his notebooks. So even though I knew he wasn't there, I asked Michael if he wanted me to pursue his writings.

It rained heavily that Saturday night, and I stopped by Sunday morning after taking Communion to a shut-in. As I approached the tombstone, I noticed that two letters of the family name PHILLIPS stood out: The *I* and the *S* appeared to be perfectly dry while all the others were dark from the rain. My first thought was "It is I." My son Chris said that "is" represents the present tense. And "is" reversed is "si," which means yes in Spanish. Before he died, Michael was studying Spanish in order to communicate with his brother's mother-in-law, who came from Colombia and was living with them.

That was my answer, then, and it was not subtle. I believe that Michael wanted his story to be told in order to share his personal relationship with a loving and caring Jesus. I believe that he wanted me to start the ball rolling. Michaels would not want to draw attention to himself, but to share examples of his personal relationship with Jesus. So I will just give you a little background on his childhood, which was fairly normal, and focus on his adulthood, including his education and work and his struggles with an alcohol addiction and an eating disorder. Michael also apparently had conversations with Jesus in the mid-nineties, which he wrote down in a journal. After this, his prayer life became absorbed in the passion of Jesus. He wrote reflections on the passion that drew on all four gospels and other sources such as *A Doctor at Calvary*. These conversations make up the bulk of this book. I have also included Michael's obituary, my funeral homily, his brother's eulogy, and an article his younger brother published in the diocesan newspaper.

Michael's Childhood

Michael was born on January 9, 1962 to George and Mary Lou (Gaffney) Phillips. He weighed 5 pounds and 10 ounces. He had colic for the first three months of his life. When he was three years old, he asked his mother who that was on the cross that hung in our living room. She said it was Jesus, who died for us. He asked her if Jesus could do magic. She said yes, you could think of the miracles as being magic. Michael replied, If Jesus had all that magic, why didn't He get Himself off the cross?

He had three brothers. Robert was a year and a half younger and a grade behind him in school. Most of the neighborhood boys were Robert's age, so Michael hung out with them, and this became his pattern—most of his friends growing up were also Robert's friends. Christopher was almost five years younger than Michael, and they became much closer when Michael returned home five years after high school. This was to be his closest friendship. George was fourteen years younger than Michael, and their friendship developed after George had graduated from college. Whenever the brothers would meet for a late breakfast or lunch, sometimes with their friends, it would generally be after the noon-day Mass and at the suggestion of Michael.

My father died suddenly on November 3, 1966, when Michael was almost five. My youngest sister had just moved away to college, so my mother was now living alone for the first time in her married life. We visited her for Thanksgiving, and as we were leaving Michael asked if he could stay with Grandma because she was alone. When Michael got older he would visit his grandmother regularly to spend a few days with her. They both cherished those moments.

When Michael was seven or eight, I took him to the Stations of the Cross on a Friday evening during Lent. As we drove home, he asked me what my favorite station was. I said I wasn't sure, but probably the fourth, in which Jesus meets His mother. He said that was his favorite too, and that it must have been very hard for His mother to see Jesus in so much pain. Michael always had a very special relationship with his own mother. As a young adult struggling with addiction and wrathfulness, he once asked his mother why God had made him. She told him that God made him to know Him, to love Him, and to serve Him in this world so that he could be happy with Him in the next.

Michael wasn't as athletic as his brothers. He did take part in their sporting endeavors, but he didn't really follow any teams in the newspaper or on TV. I started coaching youth baseball when Michael was old enough to play, and part of my reason was that I didn't want Michael playing for a hardnosed coach who would ridicule players for mistakes. Michael played little league for four years. He didn't want to continue after that, but he did help me coach.

Naturally, I was surprised that when Michael started high school, he went out for football. He even rode his bike to summer practices, seven miles each way. Needless to say, he was in excellent shape. The school didn't have freshman football, only varsity and junior varsity. Michael was on the JV team. He worried that they would sometimes have to scrimmage against the varsity team, and though he was fast he wasn't that big. Although the varsity teams were competitive, the JV teams were very weak, and the referees would usually stop games after three-quarters if they were very one-sided.

The following year, though, they had enough players for a freshmen team. Robert joined that, and Michael stayed on the JV team as a wide receiver. He had Robert throw footballs to him all summer so that he could become a better catcher and Robert a better thrower. It paid dividends, as Michael caught a lot of passes that year.

He didn't play much in his junior year, and the head coach changed for his senior year. Robert became the starting quarterback, and although Michael played defense because of his speed, they didn't throw many passes to him. It was a disappointing year because he was playing less while his younger brother was the star of the team. Michael was happy for Robert, but he was still disappointed in himself. It affected his demeanor, especially when he was drinking.

A lot of Michael's friendships developed with his fellow players. For the most part, it wasn't the popular kids but other loners like himself that Michael would befriend. They called themselves the Irregulars for that reason. And as with most teenagers, drinking became a common thing among Michael and his friends. It caused me to dread weekends and school vacations.

Michael was an excellent student. He like learning, and he liked his teachers. He didn't have a girlfriend in high school—he knew then that he was going to apply to the Franciscan seminary— but growing up, he did play with two neighborhood girls, one with whom he had a crush on. She was pretty, outgoing, and attractive, and she went to his senior prom with him even though she was a junior and had a steady boyfriend. Michael also went to the junior prom with a girl whose brother was either studying to be a priest or had already become one.

One of the highlights of Michael's high school life was a mission trip to a poor community called Nazareth Farm, in rural West Virginia. They left on a Sunday morning after celebrating Mass in the school chapel. It was one of the most emotional services I've attended. About twenty students who were going on the trip and another thirty from the Mission Club performed in the 6:00 a.m. Mass on a Sunday morning in the summer. Their final song was "Country Road." I still get goose bumps when I heard John Denver sing that song.

For his graduation, Michael wanted to hold a keg party, which was still common when the drinking age was eighteen. There were a lot of keg parties that summer, the final one being the night before he left for the seminary. I was glad that they were ending, although I was sad to see him leave home.

Education and Early Career

Michael graduated with a New York State Regents diploma from Seton Catholic Central High School in Binghamton, New York in June of 1980. He entered St. Hyacinth College in Granby, Massachusetts the following September. While there, he lived with the Franciscan community in nearby Holyoke under the direction of Father Henry and Brother Mark.

In June of 1982, he left. He spent the next year living at home, struggling with alcohol and the direction of his life. He attended Alcoholics Anonymous meetings as a condition of staying there, and he spent a month in an alcohol rehab center in Clifton Springs, New York. But when he returned, it wasn't long before he started drinking again.

In the fall of 1983, Michael applied to re-enter the Franciscan friary, which was affiliated with the Covenant House/Under 21 shelter on 460 West 41st Street in New York City, where he was volunteering full-time as a counselor's aide working with homeless youth. The first time he came home for the weekend, he told me that at Covenant House, he'd found his mission in life. The following June, he left the friary to become a full-time paid staff member. He didn't have professional training in psychiatry or sociology, but what he could offer was love.

Father Bruce Ritter, the founder and director of Covenant House, made a powerful impression on Michael, as this reflection shows:

> *Father Bruce Ritter has vitally affected my thinking. He is a Franciscan priest who works to provide shelter for homeless and runaway youth. He is an advocate for these young people and has made the public aware of the injustices they suffer. His work and ideals are an inspiration to me. He has made me aware of my responsibility to help change what is wrong in our society.*
>
> *I heard Father Bruce speak when I was in high school. Listening to him and reading about him stirred up in me a desire to become involved in serving homeless youth. I come from a good, loving, middle-class family, and it haunted me to know that so many young people suffered so much. It did not seem right to turn my back and walk away.*
>
> *After graduating, I entered the seminary of the Franciscan Order to which Father Ritter belongs. My dream was to one day work with homeless youth. The seminary was in a tough inner-city neighborhood, and while living there I became involved with some of the local people. They were often victims of poverty, drug addiction, lack of education, lack of opportunity, and broken homes. The more time I spent with them, the more their suffering bothered me. Despite their sometimes rough exteriors, I found them to be good, caring people. I was fortunate to know them.*
>
> *I left the seminary after two years and returned to my family. A year later I joined the Franciscan affiliate program and went to New York City. There I worked as a full time volunteer, and later as paid staff, at Covenant House/Under 21, a shelter for homeless youth that Father Ritter founded.*
>
> *Living in the city and working at Covenant House was an awesome experience. I worked with girls who had children or were pregnant. They taught me a lot. Despite their pain, they had so much hope and love for their children. They taught me about the dignity and sanctity of life. It was a privilege to learn from them.*
>
> *On one occasion, Father Bruce spoke with the staff about Covenant House's mission. His talk had a lasting impact on me. He challenged us to have absolute respect and unconditional love for the young people and for each other. To me, having absolute respect and love for anyone seemed impossible. It was and is merely an ideal I strive toward. But Father Bruce made the impossible seem possible by pointing out that God loves us unconditionally. We do not deserve it. He simply loves us in a special and profound way. Experiencing unconditional love is what allows us to reach our own*

potential, and with God's love this is possible.

After almost two years in the city, I was feeling homesick and returned to my family in Binghamton. I was fortunate enough to find a job at the Salvation Army Open Door Youth Shelter, which helps homeless men from 16 to 21 years old. These people are often viewed as tough and uncaring, but I've found this to be untrue. They act tough to survive, but they are often victims of our self-centered society. Working there, I've gotten to know many young men who have been hurt deeply and want to be cared about and cared for. Getting to know them has been a privilege—they have challenged me to reach my potential, and I have received far more than I have given. Working with them has enriched my life.

Father Bruce, too, has had a lasting impact on my life. I have been working with homeless youth for more than six years. I hope to continue part-time while going to school. And it was Father Bruce's message that led me to this work—his challenge, to have absolute respect and unconditional love for others, is an ideal I am striving for.

In March of 1985, Michael returned home. From July to December, he worked in a Family and Children's Society group home, where he helped provide a home-like environment to youths who were living in placement by providing them with support and guidance. In December, he started working at the Salvation Army shelter, and there he worked his way up to independent living coordinator. His responsibilities included counseling, aftercare services, referrals for appropriate services, home visits, and jail visits.

Captain Robert O. Chase, ACSW commanding officer of the Salvation Army in Binghamton, New York, wrote this recommendation for Michael on June 5, 1987:

I have known Mike Phillips for more than three years as he has been employed as a counselor aide in the Salvation Army Open Door Youth Shelter in Broome County. As agency director, I worked closely with Mike on weekends, when I was on call. Mike seeks and uses supervision appropriately, but not excessively.

Mike is a responsible person and a mature, diligent worker. He works comfortably within the agency context of practices while at the same time relating well to the troubled adolescents in our program. He has always upheld agency polices while advocating for clients through a realistic understanding of their personal goals and a genuine concern for their welfare. I have on many occasions deferred to Mike's judgment before making a decision on a crisis case. I have been impressed by his maturity and soundness of thought.

Mike is eager to please and eager to learn. He has been taking human service courses at Broome Community College while working with us, and this combination of education and practical experience will make him an asset to any organization. Your gain would be an unfortunate loss to the Army, but we understand Mike's potential for growing into positions of greater responsibility. His record of attendance, punctually, and independence in completing assignments speaks positively of him.

Michael took human services courses at Broome Community College part-time, and after two years he met with an academic advisor about what courses he needed to get his associate's degree. They looked through his transcript from St. Hyacinth seminary and determined that Broome would not give him credit for those courses, but SUNY Binghamton would. In fact, he was closer to getting a bachelor's degree in human services from Binghamton than to completing his program at Broome. So Michael switched schools and received a BS in applied social science from the School of Education and Human Development at Binghamton in June of 1991.

That December, Michael took a position as a drug and alcohol counselor with the Chemical Dependency Services Unit of the Broome County Mental Health Department, and became a credentialed alcoholism and substance abuse counselor (CASAC) in the State of New York. In 2002, he was recognized as Broome County Counselor of the Year. As a counselor, Michael could not share details of his interactions with clients, but I have no doubt that his impact on their recovery was profound. And his fellow counselors submitted many reasons for his nomination for this award:

> In a field that is relatively new, and continually changing as new theories and treatment modalities are explored, we would like to acknowledge this individual's consistencies.

> Michael subscribes to the highest ethical standards. He thoroughly and thoughtfully considers all aspects of situations to be dealt with. His regard for the total well-being of his clients is evident. Michael is non-judgmental, seeking the best in people, and meets his clientele where they are at. One may say that he epitomizes Rogerian philosophy. Michael has an enviable knack for engaging his clients. He excels at establishing rapport. He has long been known at this agency for the units of service he produces. His clients seldom miss appointments and will return to treatment specifically to work with him, as he instills a sense of trust. Michael has been willing to make personal sacrifices to continue in direct counseling with a clientele that he feels committed to.

> As a co-worker and employee, he is simply the best. He is professional, loyal, and a team player. He has been and continues to be flexible and adapts to the changes within the agency. He has wonderful interpersonal skills and always maintains a positive working relationship with all referral sources. We feel fortunate in having had an opportunity to work with him. The treatment community can always count on Michael to give his all and serve as a wonderful representative of this field; the bottom line is that Michael Phillips is a "good egg."

Michael was deeply humbled by this award. In his acceptance speech, which was very short and practiced many times, he said, "I can only accept this award on behalf of my fellow workers, who with their help made it possible. It has been an awesome privilege to get to know my clients."

Mike used Carl Rogers's "client-centered therapy" which focuses on becoming a person. This contains several key elements for a helping (therapeutic) relationship:

1. Being myself: Being my feeling and attitudes; congruence.

2. Unconditional regard for the other.

3. Empathy: Coming as close as possible to the other's experience; being non-judgmental.

4. Accepting and trying to understand another's experience as he sees it.

He felt there were two areas he especially needed to work on:

Being I: Respecting and appreciating my goodness and what I can offer; being myself with another, with a companion.

Listening: Being aware of my feelings and myself; not judging and thinking ahead; being of aware of who the other is with me.

Michael's Journals

Reflections and Explorations: 1990–1991

October 17, 1990

Trust.

Today it really hit me how little I trust. As usual, I tried to start the day with quiet, prayerful listening. I tried to be open to God. As usual, many distraction crept into my mind. I was not open but preoccupied with self-concerns and worry. I wondered what the day would be like and what I should do.

Later, walking to Mass and feeling cut off, it hit me: *trust*. Suddenly, I was thinking about my life—who and what I am and the problems (the ones I worry about so often) that I have failed to solve in my life. Trust.

When I look at my life, I see that God has been and is with me. He calls me to trust in Him and His love. He calls me to trust in His goodness. He wants me to be "me" before Him and with others. He wants me to trust others—to trust in their goodness, to nurture it. He want me to trust in my own goodness—to trust that I am created in His image, as we all are. I must face my selfish self and be I in Him. All He asks is that I trust. He will take care of me.

October 18, 1990

It is what we are excited about that educates us. —Mike Rose, *Lives on the Boundary*

Today I bought *On Becoming a Person* by Carl Rogers. George Yonemura, my counseling teacher, has made me excited about learning. Psychology has often seemed like a dry and impersonal subject to me, but George kindled my interest in Carl Rogers's philosophy of counseling.

Rogers's philosophy is based on the individual. Every person is a beautiful and precious mystery. Counseling is not a matter of diagnosing and curing, of acting as a doctor. It is a matter of being yourself for and with another person in a way that helps the other to be themselves and find their own answers to their problems—the answers that lie within them. This view calls us to see our common goodness and nurture it in each other. I'm excited to learn. This philosophy of helping very much supports my theology—what I believe God is and who I and others are in the world. I hope that I can learn so that I can be me for others.

(This is the first class I've ever taken in which I chose to read an extra book. George gave us two books to start off with and told us to read whatever else we desired).

October 20, 1990

Camouflage.

I play the game a lot. Act "cool." Be a "strong, tough man." Make fag jokes. I wish I didn't. I just want to be me. I wish I could. (Written after going out drinking on Friday night.)

Today I met with George. He is a powerful, humble, and loving teacher, counselor, and person. In the short time I've known him, he has enriched my experiences of life and being me.

A while back I wrote a story about my experience coming to terms with myself and the impact God and others have had on me. I'm happy to say that today I am glad to be me. (I have not always felt this way.) But George challenged me today. He sees me as someone good, humble, and loving. He shows great respect for the struggles and pains I've gone through. He honors me. I had trouble accepting his recognition of goodness in me—I insisted that I still have many faults. I'm still selfish. I'm still weak and imperfect. But he challenged me to accept my weaknesses and handicaps and failings and focus on what is good about me. He encouraged me to enjoy being me and not waste my energy focusing on my limitations.

What is good about me?

I am a person who has suffered much. I am "handicapped." I have known pain and loneliness, and my pain has taught me compassion. It has made me a humble person.

I have reverence, fear, and awe of God, others, life, and myself. Life is an awesome and beautiful mystery. Every person, including me, is also an awesome and beautiful mystery.

My pain forced me to face my selfish self. In doing this I realized how poor and broken I am, and in this poverty I expressed my need for God and others. I need to be loved and to love. Love brings about wholeness and unity. My heart begs for it. What a gift: hungry faith.

My faith involves quiet waiting. It calls me to listen and be open to others and to the other. My faith in God and in man's goodness leads me to be open to love. Through the grace of God and the love He has shown me through others in pain, it has healed me. It still heals me and makes me grow in love. For this I am thankful. My struggle and pain could have ended in my being bitter. I am thankful they did not, and I am thankful to be me.

October 25, 1990

Yesterday I experienced unconditional care and absolute respect from George Yonemura. His respect for me and his refusal to see me as crazy have helped me gain a new sense of respect for myself.

October 27, 1990

This is kind of hard to say, but I'm beginning to enjoy and appreciate being me. I'm not perfect, but that's ok. In my weakness, I experience my need for God. I'm starting to believe it's ok to be me. I'm glad to be me, and I enjoy being me when I am with others and when I am alone. Feeling good about being me feels funny, and it seems to be contagious. I seem to be sharing in the joy of life, the joy of being me as a part of the world.

October 28, 1990

In confession a few weeks back, Father Brown told me to just be me. I felt good about me after that—I felt that it's ok to be me. Today in Mass he said, "Life is a love affair with God." Grace is not a *thing*, but God's love pursuing us. Sin is not a thing, but a matter of being unfaithful to our lover. Pondering on my love affair with God, I believe I should start treasuring His presence, treasuring who I am, and treasuring my experience with others.

October 31, 1990

Who am I becoming?

I feel like I'm just starting to become me. I'm beginning to slow down and relax about who I am. And I'm discovering the need to slow down even more. As I slow down, I become aware of who I am. I am a student and a person who works with youth. I'm a brother, a son, a friend, an anorexic, and a Catholic. But I am more than these. I am I, and experiencing this being is good. I hope to become more open and aware of who I am. I believe that in doing this I will become more able to experience the goodness and awesomeness of life—of creation, of others, and of God. As I come to know myself better, I feel that I'm becoming a more open and loving person. It's a feeling of joy and awe, of wanting to share in the beauty of life. It is good to be me. I hope to listen more.

November 4, 1990

Today was a long day of study and work. It was long but good, too. I feel good—I'm starting to accept me and appreciate me. I want to take care of me. It's funny, but this isn't selfish at all—taking care of myself doesn't close me off from others. Rather, this taking-care-of-me opens me up to caring more about others. It's a good feeling. I can accept me as imperfect and changing.

At work, a young man stopped in to talk. He made me feel really good. I listened to him for a long time and tried to understand him. He said that he thought I was the only person who understood him. This is sad, because he's a good person. I am privileged to be getting to know him, and I hope others can too.

He compared me to other people he talks to, including professionals and psychologists, and said, "You seem to be the only one who really understands me—you don't use numbers and reasons." I took this as a compliment. I am trying to move away from judging and analyzing, to being more accepting and compassionate. This non-direct approach seems to have much more power for insight into others and myself.

It was a good experience. I am learning; he taught me. I am grateful.

November 7, 1990

Tonight I feel hope.

I am ok being I, and I will be ok by being me. I am hopeful in love. Others love me: God, my friends, and my family. Today, I experienced this—I am loved. It's funny, but I'm starting to love myself, too. Sure, I have faults and problems, but it's ok for me to be me. It actually feels pretty good.

I am tired but thankful. I hope to get a job. I hope to get better, but I'm not worried about this.

I'm beginning to trust me, God, others, and life. It feels good, and I am thankful. I'm starting to live in the moment as me, and I'm trying to experience being me to the fullest. It's an awesome experience.

November 8, 1990

I'm starting to live in the moment, to experience being me in the present. I am aware of now and not looking back or ahead. I am starting to feel feelings instead of just thinking about them. I want to write about what I'm learning—about what I'm being taught and what I'm experiencing.

Today I found experiencing myself and experiencing others to be rewarding, prayerful, and enjoyable. I spent time with two youths I've known and liked for a long time. It was great, and I really felt that they liked each other. This was much more powerful than thinking about how I like someone or how he or she likes me. I experiencing our liking each other, and I liked it. It was good.

One of the youths had been called an "antisocial type" by professionals. Some people felt there was no hope for him. My experience today made me believe differently. I changed, and I felt there was something good about this guy. He's gotten a taste of religious experience. He's started meeting with friends who discuss the Bible. It has been powerful and meaningful to him. He said, "I'm starting to really get into God, but I still have trouble with my temper." I was so happy for him. I wish him all the best, and I hope we can continue to be channels of God's healing for each other by each other.

November 10, 1990

I'm tired tonight, but it's a healthy kind of tired. I finished some job application letters and got some groceries. I spent the evening with my family, visiting an aunt and uncle—they're really beautiful people. And I finished Carl Rogers's book on becoming a person.

I'm kind of scared. My knee hurt while I was walking, so I'm trying to walk less. I'm cutting back, but I'm afraid I could have a serious problem. May God bless my knees and me—I really like to walk. It cuts down the stress and burns calories. I am trying to get well.

November 17, 1990

I broke a rib coughing on November 12 and stayed with my family until today. It was good to spend time with them. I have a job interview at Project U Uplift on November 20 at 2:30 pm. I am hopeful.

Blessed are those who are single-hearted, they shall see God.

I feel discouraged tonight. I've been reading a book by Mother Theresa. She is so single-hearted and open to God, and so aware of His presence in her life. She sees Him in others. She experiences God, she lives in love with Him, and she is not distracted.

When I look at myself I see a person who is distracted by worries, doubts, and fears. I am so weak and preoccupied with so many things that seem so important but aren't. The thought comes to me that maybe God is trying to tell me, "I am all you need, be open to my presence in your life, I love you and want to love through you and live in love with you."

Lord Jesus Christ, Son of God, Have mercy on me, a sinner.

November 18, 1990

Reading what Mother Theresa wrote has given me hope tonight. I want to be more open to God's presence within me. I want to know Him and His love and allow Him to love others through me. I hope to become single-hearted too, seeking and desiring only Him and His love. In this I will grow as a loving person.

Tuesday November 20, 1990

I feel ok. I guess I am ok. Today was rough, though. I was rejected for a job I really wanted. I don't have the skills they need. I can accept that. What hurts is the fact that there are not a lot of jobs out there. The day is done, though, and I feel more hopeful.

Chris came home from student teaching today. It hurts to see him hurt. I wish I could do something for him. I pray that he finds happiness and meaning as who he is.

November 29, 1990

Being me can be very lonely. I have allowed my handicaps to isolate me. I am afraid to be me. For the past few years I've been taking "baby steps" toward living a more meaningful life. I've come a long way, but I have a long way to go. I'm tired but hopeful, fearful yet thankful. People are so precious. Opening up and getting to know others enriches me, but so often I pull back in fear—I run away from closeness. I need to slow down and be open.

December 3, 1990

I'm stressed out tonight. I feel unsure about my career decisions. Should I try to go back to the youth shelter, or get a job with Catholic Charities? I've talked it over with my family and have been thinking about it a lot. I'd rather have the shelter job, but I'm not sure if I should wait for it. Four weeks of looking and applying for jobs has been discouraging. My brother tells me to trust my gut feeling. That means going back to the shelter.

December 8, 1990

Tonight I'm tired, sick, and stressed out. I think I re-broke my rib, and my back is hurting from moving food at work yesterday. I'm angry too—I felt used at work. It was my own fault, though. I don't express myself. I could have said, "I can't do all of this heavy lifting. I'm recovering from a broken rib." But I'm afraid to do that because it's my own fault that my rib is broken and that I'm in poor health. I'm anorexic and I don't take care of myself.

Oh God, help me to take care of myself. Forgive me for blaming others for my pain. Help me pray. Help me get to know You better and become open to Your way, as St. Anthony of the Desert was. Help me enjoy my relationship with You, and help me be thankful that You are with me. You became like one of us so that we might become like You. You are the "Bread of Life." You are my life. Thanks.

January 8, 1991

Tonight while reading *Crime and Punishment*, I was struck by the question in the Gospel of John, in the story of the raising, when Jesus says, "I am the Resurrection and the Life." It filled me with hope. I hope to find that my life is in God and to understand that life is awareness of Him being present to me.

Last week, on New Year's Day, I got sick for the first time in two years.

I offer You me. I desire to please You. You are my God and my all. May I love You and see You in others and love them.

February 10, 1991

Tomorrow I get the results of my AIDS test. I am scared. I don't remember having sex with anyone, but I have many of the symptoms of AIDS. Could I have had sex during one of the two blackouts I had in New York City when I was drinking?

I'm scared. God, help me. Help me to desire and seek to please You by the life I live, at work, rest, play, and prayer. May I seek to know You and make Your love known. Help me. I binged today, and last night, and I'm scared about tomorrow. Please help me to begin again.

February 19, 1991

Today I saw another doctor. My lymph nodes are swollen. I have the symptoms of AIDS, and I'm scared. My HIV test came back negative, which means I probably don't have it, but if I do it's so bad that it doesn't register on the test. The doctor said that the chance I have it is about one in a hundred. Oh God, help me. Oh God, be merciful to a sinner.

February 22, 1991

Detachment.

Oh God, I am so attached to so much. I offer You my attachments. Help me become detached and open to You. Thank You.

February 27, 1991

Today was a rough one. I am sick, and I spent the day binging on cereal and fruit. (At least it's not fattening.) I am stressed out and worried, and I take it out by overeating. I am scared and tired of waiting. I am terrified that I have AIDS. The doctor is supposed to get back to me soon, but it's been more than a week. I have the symptoms, but my test was negative, but I still could have it—the disease may have progressed to the point that the test doesn't pick it up.

To the best of my knowledge, I have never had sex with anyone. The only way I think I could have gotten AIDS was if I did something (or someone did something to me) on a night when I had a blackout—one in New York City, one in Staten Island. Why did I have to drink so much? It might have cost me my life. The blackout in NYC happened when I was a volunteer at the Franciscan Friary. I learned later that another volunteer had "put me to bed," and I have reason to think he may have been gay. Could something have happened?

I'm terrified, sick, and tired. Oh God, have mercy on me, a sinner.

March 9, 1991

God, help me to have a growing awareness of You in my life. Thanks.

Thursday Mar 28, 1991, Holy Thursday

Thank You, God. I'm ok. My biopsy said that I'm just recovering from s-virus, similar to mono.

At the Last Supper, You called us to "Do this in memory of Me." Help me to give myself, the way You gave yourself as bread for others in the Eucharist. It is in giving myself that I remember You. You are presence in self-sacrificing love.

April 12, 1991

I saw something special today. It made me feel good and yet sad.

This was a rough week at work—lots of hurting kids. I took two of them grocery shopping in the van, and on our way back they caught sight of another kid who used to live with them at the shelter. He had been put in the psychiatric ward at the hospital—by me and the police—because he was suicidal, and now he was walking around downtown with a staff member of the hospital. The two kids went crazy, they were so excited, so I let them out of the van and they took off to see him.

This was when it really hit me. To everyone else, they're misfits. But they have something special. They are united as people, when so often we are so divided in our high-class world. They showed me what it is like to really be loved. They experienced brotherhood together. Maybe they aren't really the misfits. What a privilege it is to be a part of their lives and to get to know them.

Jesus, help me to be still and to come to know the mystery of Your love in me. Help me to trust in Your loving care.

May 5, 1991

Today I am overwhelmed, discouraged, and depressed by my helplessness, by my inability to deal with my sickness, weakness, and sinfulness. I try but I fail. Life is a struggle, and it feels like more than I can handle. At times I feel like a dog—a reject, a misfit, and a pretty miserable one. My day-to-day life is a struggle.

I need a savior. Jesus, have mercy on me, a sinner.

I do not deserve to be loved by You. I am not worthy of Your forgiveness. It's hard to believe You love me. How could You who are so good love me, a sick, ugly and sinful man?

Help me to accept and be open to the mystery and glory of Your love. You who are God suffered and died for us all, especially for me, even though none of us deserves such limitless and unconditional sacrificial love. I am sorry for being so closed and untrusting toward You. Grant me the grace to slow down and open up to You, to be aware that You are with me, You who are my God and Savior. Thanks.

July 27, 1991

You should not be working for perishable food but for food that remains unto life eternal, food which the Son of Man will give you.

God, thanks for the gift You have given me. Thanks for the gifts of generosity, compassion, faith, understanding, gentleness, and the desire for You and for love. These are the gifts You have given me—an unworthy sinner. Help me to see that any good that I have or do comes from You. Your gifts reflect you. May I see Your gift in others too.

I offer You what You have given me. Receive me to do what you will. May I use the gifts You have given me to give You glory and make You known in the world. Thanks. I love you.

June 9, 1993

I do believe. Help my lack of faith.

The last entry I made in this book was two years ago. My life has changed—You have been with me—and I'm still hanging in there. After fourteen years, I'm still struggling with my sickness. The past few weeks have been some of the worst. Sickness, worry, and stress are wearing me out, and I feel lost, I feel like a failure. Today, due to work responsibilities, I couldn't get to Mass. But while I was taking a cigarette break, standing alone and wishing I had made it, it hit me—You are always with me. Maybe life has been so difficult lately because I haven't been as open, aware, and trusting as You call me to be.

Lord, help me believe that You are always with me. Help me turn my life over to You. Grant me this gift of the spirit so that I might serve You in a world full of people who are starving for Your love. Help me trust in Your limitless, unconditional, personal love for me. With You, I have hope and strength. Thanks.

Dialogue 1: 1994–1995

June 15, 1994

Love your enemies. Be made perfect as your heavenly Father is perfect.

Jesus, I fall so short at Your gospel call—the challenge to love unconditionally and to give of myself limitlessly, as You did and still do. I'm weak and sinful. There is so much in me that blocks me from being made perfect. Have mercy on me and grant me the grace I need to overcome the obstacles within me that stop me from getting to know You.

Friday, November 18, 1994

Trust Me. Be open to Me and My love. I AM with you. You are sick and broken, you need Me, and I AM here for you.

Thanks for the really good sleep. Thanks for touching me through my brother's compassionate hope. He reflects Your love and hope for me. Thanks for loving me and for the hope You have given me.

I'm scared of dying, but it's a possible outcome of my sickness. I still feel shielded by numbness, but reality is slowly sinking in, and I'm sad and afraid. I also feel guilty—somehow my anorexia is my own fault, and I'm hurting those who love me and I'm hurting myself. But maybe I'm just play Monday-morning quarterback pondering what I should have done—the past cannot be undone.

It's becoming obvious that my life is at stake. Fear and anxiety grip my gut, yet hope is dawning. You, Lord are my hope, and through Your grace I'm slowly beginning to change. Help me to progress, little by little. I feel guilty because I feel I should make "big, radical changes." This is a nice thought, but as an anorexic, it just doesn't fit me. Going too fast, too far, too soon could cause the "binge monster" to come back, and I fear him—the viscous binge–purge cycle—almost as much as I fear death. The cycle is a living hell. Lord, I hope that making small, consistent changes will be enough to keep me alive. Perhaps the answer is learning to live with my problem and with myself.

Guide me and protect me, O Most Holy Son of God. Help me listen to You and respond. Thanks.

Jesus, have mercy on me, a sinner. I trust in You.

Love, Mike

December 6, 1994

People came to hear Him and be healed.

Blest are you poor—the reign of God is yours.

Come to Me, be in My loving presence. I AM with and in you, I AM healing you, and I will give you rest. Trust Me.

Dear Lord,

Help me tonight to trust in you. I'm a sinful and sick and exhausted man. I'm having trouble sleeping—too much anxiety. Change and growth are good but painful. I will be seeing the doctor Thursday, and the last of my health worries will be confronted. I'm either ok, or I've done some severe damage to my body.

Receive me tonight, Lord. Help me to trust in You. You are my salvation. In my poverty and brokenness, I'm beginning to know my need for You. Thanks for teaching and healing me.

Love, Mike.

December 12, 1994

Dear Lord,

Thanks for three years at the Drug Awareness Center. Thanks for the pain that is leading to growth—to nutrition, caring for myself, getting close to my family, and becoming more aware of my need for You.

Help me trust You and turn my life over to You. You want to call me to love You, others, and myself. Please grant me the grace to change, to become in love. Help me be open to Your healing love. Thanks. And please help too with my sleeping. Grant me rest in you—I'm getting worn out, and I'm sick. I offer my pain to You and trust Your will. Please help me to surrender more and trust more. Thanks. I love You.

Love, Mike

January 16, 1995

Letter to the little child within me.

Dear Little Mike,

For years I have been cruel to you, calling you bad, ugly, evil, and worthless, out of guilt and shame for my anger and fear and jealousy. I have taken my feelings out on you, and you never deserved it. I am sorry to have hurt you so badly. You are wounded and sick, and you are half of me, too.

We need help. I am working to take better care of myself. Please help me stop paying attention to you. You are special, beautiful, and gentle, and I want very much to go back to being a beautiful child made in the image of God's Son. I hope and pray with His grace that I can give you the love you deserve and make up for so many years of deceit. Please forgive me.

Your big brother, Mike.

January 18, 1995

Tonight I'm scared. I'm worried about my liver and about sleep. Help me to relax and sleep and trust You with my anxiety and health. You will take care of me. Thanks.

January 19, 1995

Tonight I'm nervous. I'm scared about my liver and worried about my brother having to move on us. Lord, I offer us to You. Help me to trust in You. Thanks.

January 20, 1995

I'm exhausted tonight—tight stomach, nausea, stress about my brother. Jesus, our crucified savior and God, You are with us. Save us, have mercy on us, and grant us peace of mind. Thanks.

January 21, 1995

Thanks for last night and today.

January 22, 1995

Thanks for last night and today. I'm nervous, scared, worried, but hopeful for my brother. Help me be open to You and Your healing, and have mercy on us. Thanks.

January 23, 1995

Rough day at the office. I'm exhausted, tired, and worried about my health. Christ, You are my Savior. Thanks for getting me through. Help me to trust and be open to You. Thanks.

January 24, 1995

Thankful, hopeful, wanting to trust. I believe in Your healing, but I'm also worried about hemorrhoids, liver, sleep, hospital, brother. I'm scared and anxious. Help me to trust in Your mercy, love, and healing. Have mercy on us all. Thanks.

January 25, 1995

Nervous, anorexic, tired, scared. Health, sleep, brother. Have mercy, grant me trust in You, my Savior.

January 27, 1995

Thanks for hope and for healing. Help me find hope in Your love. I'm a little nervous, anxious, worried, scared. About my health and my brother. Have mercy on us, Lord. Thanks.

Lord, I am exhausted. I am scared, angry, lonely, and hurting. I offer You myself, the good, the bad, and the ugly. I'm a sinner, and I need You. I'm a very sick person, and I need You. I depend on You to help me to get back—body, mind, and soul.

January 28, 1995

I'm anxious, nervous, guilty, ashamed, and exhausted, yet I'm hopeful. I often give thanks for Your being our Savior and Lord. You have received my causes about my health, physical and spiritual, and about my family, especially my brother.

January 30, 1995

Forgive me. I feel guilty. I lied to Helen. I don't want to gain pounds. And I'm scared.

Do not condemn and you will not condemned.

Forgive me and heal me. Help me open up and give me the grace to change.

January 31, 1995

Thanks for Your forgiveness, healing, and peace. Thank You for sleep. Thank You for helping my family. I am still scared and anxious. I love You. Please have mercy on us.

I'm sorry that I lied. I'm sick. Forgive me, I know I need to change, or I'll end up in the hospital. I'll end up losing my job, my life, and the path You have set me on and the vocation You have called me to. I am scared yet hopeful, and now I can feel better, not gain weight, and be healthier.

February 3, 1995

Mike, I want you to know Me and how much I love you.

Lord, You once prayed "Father, forgive them." Thanks for Your effort, sacrifice, and gift. You offered forgiveness, healing, reconciliation, union, and peace. Receive my anxiety and worries. I am scared, sinful, and preoccupied with my cares and family. Help me to trust in You and be open to the life You have for me. Lord have mercy on us. Thanks.

February 4, 1995

Mike, I desire to forgive and heal and love you and reveal myself to you.

Lord, forgive me for being so selfish. Heal me, body, mind, and soul. Thanks for today, thanks for my family, and thanks for Bob and Alice. I love You. Have mercy on us.

February 5, 1995

Mike, be united to Me. Experience Me in communion and love.

Lord, help me to be open to You. Thanks.

February 6, 1995

Mike I desire to share My life with you—My Passion, Death, Resurrection. Trust, be open, and know that I am your lover, savior, and God.

Lord, I'm sick, tired, scared, anxious, crazy —help me to trust in You receive me in my brokenness, Thanks.

February 7, 1995

Mike, I love to have you enter into My love, the Passion mystery. Be open to My spirit.

Lord, thanks for helping me. Continue to reveal Yourself to the world and to me. Thanks. I love You. Have mercy on us.

February 8, 1995

This is My body, to be given for you. This cup is the new covenant of My blood, which will be given for you.

Mystery. I gave you Myself and My life, My flesh and blood. I who am true God and man, your savior, I gave My life for you. I did this that you might share in My life. I love you immensely, I thirst for you.

Lord, I offer You my life's problems, that You might receive them and heal me. My anger, sadness, fear, anxiety, confusion, doubt, and guilt. Receive me in my boredom, sickness, and selfishness. Thanks.

Grant me help. I love You. Have mercy on us.

February 9, 1995

This is My body, to be given to you. I love you, I am with you, and I will take care of you. Trust Me.

Lord, I am sick and scared tonight. I am worried, fearful of the hospital, sleep, the bathroom, eating, my health, my guilt, my embarrassment, and my family. Receive me tonight, body, mind, and soul, and grant me Your help. Thanks for the gift of Yourself. Help me to be open to You. I love You. Have mercy on me. Have mercy on us.

Take this and eat it. This is My body, to be given for you. Do this as a remembrance of Me. They crucified Me. Forgive them.

Reach out, despite your pain, and do what I did. Show who you are. Be open to My forgiveness, healing, and love, and share them with others.

Lord, forgive me for being so caught up in me. Grant me the grace to reach out to others even when I am tired. I love You. Have mercy on us.

February 10, 1995

I greatly desire to give myself to you, My body and blood, for forgiveness, healing, and union. Be open to receive me. Surrender to my love.

Lord, receive me tonight, help me surrender. Thanks for loving me so much. I love You. Have mercy on us.

February 11, 1995

Do this in remembrance of Me.

Lord make me a channel of Your peace. Grant me the grace to reach out. Forgive me for my selfishness and for being caught up in my own worries and guilt, using my family and myself. Help me to be better in Your will, to surrender, be open, and be a channel of Your love.

Thanks. I love You. Have mercy on me.

February 13, 1995

Do this in remembrance of Me.

Lord, You literally gave Yourself to me today, and You are in me. Help me to remember that You are my Savior.

Thanks, I love You. Have mercy on us and on me.

February 14, 1995, Valentine's Day

Take and eat this. It is My body, given for you. I am with you. Be open to me in the sacrament of Mine. Receive me daily. I love you immensely.

Lord, receive my troubles tonight. Help me be open to You so that I can love. Thanks for accepting me as I am. I offer You me tonight. I love You. Have mercy on us.

February 15, 1995

Do this in remembrance of me. Be open to Me. Slow down and live in the moment. Be happy and rejoice in my love for you.

I feel anxious tonight. I get results on my liver tomorrow. I'm scared. Of the hospital, of eating, of the bathroom, of smoking. I hope to be ok. I feel thankful, too, though. For a good day, for work and food. And I'm very tired. I'm hopeful that I can get a good night's rest. I'm worried, too. Phone calls and family, work schedule, guilt that I didn't call Alice.

Receive my failings tonight, and help me to be open to You, my God, my savior. You Who are with me and love me as I am. Thanks for getting me through. I love You. Have mercy on us.

Help me to believe, trust, and reach out and laugh.

February 16, 1995

This is My body, to be given up for you. I am with you and I am in you. Don't be afraid. I am your food and nourishment. Open up to My healing love, and you will find life and rest.

Tonight, I am grateful. The ultra-sound was ok. I'm still worried about my liver enzymes not being quite right. Will retest in March. I'm worried of getting sick, about the hospital, about eating, sleeping, smoking, bathroom, and death. I'm also worried about my brother and about sleep.

It makes me sad to think what I've done to myself. I'm angry at myself, and tired, but I'm beginning to grow and be more flexible. It feels good, and I increased my food today by just a little.

Help me, Lord. Receive me and my feelings. Grant me the grace to be patient, to live in the moment and love in the moment, and to continue one small step at a time, knowing that You are with me. Thanks too for letting me have laughter and people to love and be loved by. Thanks. I love You. Have mercy on all of us.

February 17, 1995

They crucified him.

Food I gave you Myself, love and forgiveness. I did this because I greatly desire you to know Me. Silence. Be open and still—I am with you.

Lord, thanks for being with me in my fears and anxieties. I love You. Thanks.

February 18, 1995

This is My body, to be given for you.

They crucified him.

I am with you and in you—I am your crucified lover, lord redeemer, healer, and God. Open up to my healing love. I am healing you. Believe. I want to have you know me and my love for you so very much. Listen.

Lord, receive me tonight. I am sick, scared, helpless, powerless, doubtful, sinful, and afraid. I need saving and help. Forgive me for all I have done, heal my brokenness, and help me turn my life around to You. Help me let go and surrender. Have mercy on us. Thanks, Lord, for helping and answering my prayers. I love You.

Tonight I am wiped out. For the third time in three weeks, my hemorrhoids are bleeding. My anxiety is overwhelming. How can I make it? Will I end up in the hospital? It's scary. I need to change, to make small steps toward getting better. Perhaps I am too hard on myself. Maybe I need to slow down and take smaller steps, be realistic and not get depressed. I need to accept who I am, what I am: a sinner, a sick man who needs help.

You, o Lord, are there for me and with me, slowly healing me to prepare me for Yourself. Help me to surrender, to learn from the cross. Teach me and guide me, Lord. Continue to heal me and know how dependent I am on You. Without You, I have no hope. With You, I have it all.

February 19, 1995

The cup is the new covenant of My blood, which will be shed for you.

I shed My blood on the cross for you. I am your crucified lord, God, love, and savior. I call you into a covenant and a relationship of love. I give you Me and My life. Be open to Me and My limitless love for you.

Thanks, Lord, for shedding Your blood for us all. You are our savior. I pray to You, Most Glorious God. Receive my thanks tonight. You have helped me with my exhaustion, work, fear, and anxiety. You have helped my health, my sleep, and my brother. Have mercy on us. I love You.

Mike, I invite you to a new relationship, one of total surrender. Be thankful and rejoice. I love you, I am with you, and I shed My blood so that you might be able to live in union with Me.

February 20, 1995

This cup is the new covenant in My blood to be shed for you.

February 21, 1995

Mike, slow down and give thanks in all things. Learn to surrender to My loving care for you and others. I call you to a holy relationship with me, a loving unity. I call you to enter into the passion, into the Paschal mystery, and be transfigured. I offer you My life.

Lord, thanks. Receive me tonight (this morning). I am stressed, and I can't sleep (probably from the juice). It is my own doing catching up with me. I need saving. I am a sinner and am sick physically, emotionally, and spiritually. Thanks for opening me to Your holy love, and help me come to be more aware of my dependence on You.

I am worried about my hemorrhoids—help me be patient. Thanks for helping me. I worry a lot about my brother—he seems so broken, and I want to see him get better. Help me to trust Your loving care for him. You are with him. Help him even more than me, please. Help me let go of what I want and simply pray, love, and trust.

I am worried about whether I should visit my brother in Connecticut during Holy Week. Lots will be going on, and it may be too soon. I might wait six weeks and take a vacation day. I would prefer to save up and get money for CRS. Help me let go. I can save a day next year. Holy Week would be too much stress, too soon. I need to spend a week with You. Help me and guide me.

I'm sorry about the distraction in my prayer—it's my sickness hurting me. I blame myself and feel guilty—it's my sin. Forgive me for beating myself up, but I am sick. I need to forgive and love myself. Help me value who I am—one who was made in Your image by Your Father, and a temple of the Holy Spirit. I am awfully hard on myself. Help me to be patient and content. I am sick and broken and sinful but loveable.

Grant me the grace to accept my sickness, to accept myself as I am and others as they are, and to surrender to Your loving care. Grant me the grace to continue making small changes, and grant me the grace to be thankful in all things. And I surrender my love to You, God and Savior. Thanks. I love You.

Lord have mercy on us and on me.

The cup is the new covenant of My blood, which will be shed for you. I offer you Me and My life.

Lord, receive me tonight, tired, anxious, and angry, yet blessed. Yes, I have problems with myself, with my health and my hemorrhoids, and also with my brother, and I'm sorry for my anger with myself and my life. Forgive me. My problems are myself and my environment. You only want to love me. Help me to trust in You.

Thanks. I love You. Have mercy on us.

February 22, 1995

Help me to see that what I want for myself and others is often not the best. Your way, Your will, is the only path to wholeness for each of us. Yet it is scary—I think that I know what is better, and I struggle with being in control. Help me to trust and let go.

Thanks. I love You. Have mercy on me, a sinner. I need You.

Mike, I died to offer salvation to you and the world. I call you to experience the new covenant between God and man—Me, My life, My blood. I call you to a deeper love. Let go and surrender to Me and My love for you.

Lord, Thanks. My day was rough, but You got me through it. I feel hopeful—less sore, scared, worried, angry, and guilty (for not being with my family). More hopeful and relieved. Grant me the grace to continue to know how much I need You. Help me be open to letting go and turning my life over to You.

Thanks. I love You. Have mercy on me and us all, especially my brother.

February 23, 1995

Mike, I died for you. I love you and want what is best for you. Open up to Me and My Love for you.

Dear Lord,

I am resistant. I am exhausted from fighting and aging and living. My hems are acting up, and I'm anxious at waiting a week and a half for taxes. I'm worried about all my health problems, especially my exhaustion, yet my problems are my own doing. I can't continue to destroy my body and be obsessed with my weight.

I need to change. You can change me. I am sorry for being so resistant. I am not honestly ready to let go of my anorexia. I'm sick in the head, and it's scary. I feel that I am losing control, attention, and the payoff of weighing in. Help me see that only You will satisfy my brokenness. I need to address my anorexia, to be able to let it go and open up to You. But I am scared.

You are my God and savior. Continue to give me the grace of self-awareness, of Your will. Open me to new, small changes. Thanks for the grace that lets me make slow, tiny steps toward healing physically, emotionally, and spiritually. You will guide me and continue to help me. You have cared for this broken world by shedding Your blood and dying on the cross.

Thanks. I offer myself to You tonight, broken, sinful, yet hopeful that You will have mercy on us all, especially my brother and mother. Thanks for answering my call from the depths. I love You.

Mike.

February 24, 1995

I love you very much. Look at the cross.

Mike, slow down, open up, and trust. Let go, and let Me show you My love for you. I am your crucified, God, savior, friend, and lover.

Lord, help me to trust, to slow down, to listen, and to open up to You. Thanks for healing me, body, mind, and soul. Thanks for receiving my feelings tonight—my anxiety, fear, shame, and guilt, about my health, my sleep, my brother.

Thanks. I love You. Have mercy on us all.

February 25, 1995

Lord, thanks for the good sleep. I'm up now and can't get back to sleep, but maybe that's good. I need to work on a lot of stuff.

One step at a time with You. You call me to let go and surrender to You and Your love for me. I offer You myself tonight. I am a broken person. I don't even feel like a man. It hurts. I'm ashamed of who I am. And I have gotten very sick, physically and mentally, from not doing everything that makes up who and what I am. I guess I'm not *bad*, but I'm ugly.

I've spent my life trying to hide—behind a football hero, a drinker, a socialite, a religious person, a monk, an anorexic—and I've failed. I am ugly and have tried to hide it. I am all caught up in me. I am scared, hurt, and ashamed. I've been so mean, and I've hurt so many people, Your holy people, and my family and myself. I'm sorry and would like to say, "I'll never do this again—I'll change." But I'm scared to change, and I don't know if I want to. I just want to be loved.

Mike, I love you. I died for you. You are slowly opening up to Me and My love. Slow down, relax. I am with you and love you. I'm your savior. You can depend on Me. Call on Me. Call on Me every step of the way. Listen to Me and know My love for you.

Mike, let go of all that stands between Me and you, one step at a time.

Lord, receive me tonight, happy and thankful. You are teaching me and healing me to love. Receive my worries, too—hems (better), health, sleep, and brother.

Thanks. I love You. Have mercy on us all.

February 26, 1995

The Son of Man is following His appointed course.

Mike, slow down, open up, and listen. I will lead you on your appointed career if you let Me. This is My Father's will for you. Trust Me to lead you. I love you very much.

Lord, receive me tonight. I'm very thankful for Your help. How great Thou art.

At the same time, I struggle with worry, anxiety, and fear. I want my way for me and my brother. I hope to accept You as my lover and gentle leader. Help me surrender. I offer You myself tonight, Lord, up and down and in between me.

February 27, 1995

The Son of Man is following His appointed course. I am in your mind, the one who saves you

Mike, surrender to me and My way of love and service.

Lord, receive me tonight, a sinner and a worrier but healthy. Receive my fears. Grant me the grace to let go and trust in Your way for me. Thanks for being my savior and helping me. Grant me the grace to change and follow so that I can come to know Your love. Help me open up and let go to reach the freedom Your way offers.

I will free you of your sin and anxiety. Let go and follow My love for you.

Simon, Simon, listen to Me. I have prayed for you that you may not lose faith.

February 28, 1995

Mike, Mike, listen to Me. You will be tested. I will pray for you that you may not lose faith.

Lord, thank You. Two thousand years ago, You spoke to Peter of his betrayal. You loved him as he was even though You knew he would abandon You. Thanks for speaking to me and being present to me today, in Your word and in an extra special way.

Help me this Lent to spend time listening to You, as You speak to me in Your gospel of love. You are present. Before Your passion, You did not stop loving. You did not allow Yourself to get stuck in Your head, as I often do, but You reached out to Peter in loving compassion. Lord, help me stop getting caught up in my own head, worrying about food, health, routine, family, and everything else. Help me reach out to others and become more flexible, trusting that You will give me the grace I need for being grateful for the pain, the dependence, of knowing You more.

Tonight I am grateful. My routine and my rigidity are being changed, and You are giving me the grace to make it. Thanks for the opportunity to grow. Thanks again for speaking and being present and loving me in Your Holy Word. Forgive me for not having proper love and reverence for Your presence in Your word and for being so selfish. Receive my many fears about health, food, sleep, and my brother. Thanks for helping me trust and for giving me freedom in trust, in knowing You will take care of me.

Thanks again. I love You. Have mercy on us.

March 1, 1995, Ash Wednesday

You in turn must strengthen your brothers. I am ready to face imprisonment and death. You have thrice denied you know Me.

Mike, I AM with you and know you are not perfect, yet still I call you to depend on Me, and to let go and reach out to your brothers.

Mike, Mike, listen to Me. I will pray for you that you may not lose faith. Despite your faults, sins, and sickness, I call you to strengthen your brothers and sisters. Give yourself as I have given Myself—moment by moment. I AM with you, and I am especially present to you in My word and the gift of My body and blood.

Open up, slow down, and be reverent. I AM God, your savior and best friend, and I will give you nourishment for your struggles. Be thankful in all things, especially suffering, which challenges you to grow in dependence on Me.

(A mediation on the Last Supper—Peter's denial.)

Lord, receive me tonight, tired, anxious, worried, and scared. I fear for my health, sleep, eating, and family, yet I am grateful to You for healing me, for helping me to be flexible, and for giving Yourself to me, an unworthy sinner, in the Eucharist and in Your Word. Forgive me for being selfish and distracted by what I want. Help me to let go and be guided by You. You love me very much and call me to know You. Grant me the grace to slow down, open up to You, revere You, and reach out to others. Thanks, thanks, thanks.

I love You. Have mercy on me and all of us.

March 2, 1995

"I do not know Him."

The Lord looked at Peter. Peter remembered at once what the Lord had said, and he went out and wept bitterly.

Lord,

I am often like Peter in that I deny You. I deny You by refusing to spend time with others. I am so selfish and caught up in me and my problems—forgive me. Grant me a true spirit of repentance, the power to be sorry, to weep and open myself to Your way and Your grace so that I will have the strength to change, to let go and reach out to others.

I'm disappointed in myself because I've messed up my life so much, because I've wasted so much time and the life You have given me. Forgive me. Grant me the grace to continue to make small changes.

Thanks. I love You. Have mercy on us.

Love, Mike

Mike, I did not give up on Peter—I loved him. I will not give up on you—I love you and I AM there for you. Let go and open up to Me.

March 3, 1995

Lord, I am ready to die with You. You will say I do not know You.

I know you, Mike. I know you are weak and sick and a sinner, and I love you even more, believe Me.

Lord, forgive me for my pride. I think I know it all, but I don't know what is best for me. You know better than I. You know my good, bad, and ugly and You still love me deeply. Thanks for Your understanding and Your patient love.

March 4, 1995

They crucified him.

I solemnly assure you, this day you will be with me.

Mike, I love you spending time with me. I delight in you. I am with you and in you, and I love you. Peace.

Lord,

Wow, what a great day. Thanks for speaking to me. It's so good to know that You delight in my efforts and have so much hope for me and my job. As I carry my cross one step at a time, help me to see that You are with me. Receive my worries tonight about health, food, distractions, sleep, and especially my brother. Have mercy on him in a special way tonight. Take into Your hands my worries, cares, and hopes.

Thanks for loving me so much. Have mercy on my brother, me and all of us.

Love, Mike

March 5, 1995

Don't be terrified. You are looking for Jesus, who was crucified. He is risen. He is not here.

Every eye should see Him they have pierced.

I am the Alpha and the Omega, Who is, Who was the Almighty.

Mike, rejoice. I am your crucified and almighty savior. I am with you, and I am saving you for Me. I love you so very much.

Lord,

I praise You tonight, my Crucified, Almighty Savior. Help me to let go of my fears, anxiety for my health and my brother, and open up to You, Glorious God, my best friend and savior.

Thanks. Have mercy on us. I love You. Glory to You, Most Holy God.

Love, Mike

March 6, 1995

You will deny that you know Me.

Mike, I know you, and I accept you as you are. I love you because you are you. Like Peter, you are not perfect. You are weak and sinful, and you struggle and fall. This is ok. Keep getting back up and return to Me. Don't be so hard on yourself and others. Rely on Me more, and on My grace, and less on yourself. Seek growth and repentance. I want to be your personal savior and lover, and I want you to experience my forgiveness and healing.

Lord,

Forgive me for so often denying that I know You, especially when I reject others and close myself off from them. Grant me the grace to see You more in my daily life, and help me believe in and experience the healing power of Your transforming, limitless, and personal forgiveness and love for me. Thanks, Lord.

And please receive my feelings tonight, my worries about health, sleep, food, and family. Into Your hands I offer myself, with my hopes, worries, and fears, because I know You will give me the grace I need to continue following Your call. Thanks for calling me, loving me, and forgiving me.

Thanks. I love You. Have mercy on us all.

Love, Mike

P.S. Lord, I have lots of problems. I'm worried about being able to sleep and go to the bathroom. I'm scared, and I know I have to change my eating routine, but I don't want to gain weight—I like losing, it's a natural high. I know this is sick, but it's truly how I feel, and it scares me because it's so twisted. I'm a twisted and broken person, yet You love me for who I am, not for what my problem is. Thanks. I'll be ok.

March 7, 1995

I am your crucified savior. I am with and in you. Accept Me as your savior.

Lord, I can't make it without You. I'm too weak.

Help me to accept You in my heart as my personal lord, God, savior, best friend, and lover.

Thanks. I love You. Have mercy on us.

March 8, 1995

Don't be afraid. A savior is born for you, your messiah and lord.

Mike, accept Me into your heart as your personal, individual lord, God, lover, and savior. Slow down and listen. I AM in you.

Lord,

I'm worn out tonight, worried about fasting for my doctor's appointment. Help me to let go and rely on You. I can't make it on my own, and I need to make time, slow down, and open up to the experience of You as my personal God and savior. I'm sick, but I'm getting better.

Thanks. I love You. Have mercy on us.

Love, Mike

March 9, 1995

. . . they arrested Jesus . . .

It was our weakness that He carried and our suffering He endured. He was pierced for our offenses and crushed for our sins. Upon Him was the punishment that makes us whole.

Mike, I AM with you and know you are stressed and worn out. I took up My cross for you and everyone. I took on your suffering, weakness, and sin. I AM the sacrificial paschal Lamb. I gave My life for you that you might be made whole.

Trust Me—I'll get you through the next 24 hours of fasting. Be open to me, one moment and one step at a time, in the sacrament of love. I AM with you and in you. I AM your loving savior. You can count on Me.

Lord,

Thanks for revealing Yourself to me. What an awesome gift You made, and what a terrible price You faced and to defeat our weakness and sins. You took on the punishment I deserved because You love me. Thanks.

Receive me and my feelings, my anxiety, worry, fear, depression, and anger. Life is too much for me, but I'm seeing that this is ok. It's how it should be, because it leads me to know my need for You.

Thanks. I love You. Have mercy on us—I can make it with You.

Love, Mike

March 10, 1995

It was our weakness He bore. He was pierced for our sins. Upon Him was the punishment that makes us whole.

Mike, I am with you and in you. I love you.

Lord,

Thank You. Sacrificial Lamb of God, Lord, Savior, and Son of God, You took on my wickedness and sins and died for me. You are my savior.

Thanks for getting me through the hospital ordeal—You took on my pain and healed me. I place myself in Your loving Hands.

Thanks. I love You. Have mercy on us.

Love, Mike

March 11, 1995

. . . then bowing his head he died . . .

I died for you. I took your brokenness and sins to the cross and suffered for you that you might be offered wholeness. I am with you. Offer yourself to Me. I love and want you for myself.

Lord,

Thanks. Receive me tonight. You saved me, step by step, through Your love. Help me to listen, and remove my fears about health, sleep, and family.

Thanks. I love You. Have mercy on us.

Love, Mike

March 12, 1995

Mike, I AM your risen lord, I AM your God, I AM with you. Open up. Listen. I love you.

Be forgiven. Be open to the Holy Spirit. I offer you life. You will come to know Me, your risen and crucified lord and savior.

Lord,

Receive me tonight. I am broken, embarrassed, and ashamed. I feel like crap. It hurt to hear my friend tell my brother that I have anorexia. I've hurt and embarrassed my family and I am really struggling. It's overwhelming, I offer my worries to You, my risen lord.

I love You and need You. Have mercy on us.

Love, Mike

March 13, 1995

I will take care of you. I love you, Mike.

Jesus, after dying You were buried yet You rose from the dead. You won.

March 14, 1995

Peter said, I do not know Him.

The soldiers made fun of and beat Jesus.

Lord, I have often failed to recognize You, as Peter and the soldiers did. Sometimes I am not open and aware, but other times I simply choose to deny You. Forgive me for all the times I've been closed to You and to others and caught up in my own head.

I have wasted much of what You have given me, and I'm sorry. Please forgive me too for the times I've made fun of You and beat You by hurting my brothers, in so many ways. Give me the grace to open up to Your forgiveness and love You. Receive my anxiety, guilt, shame, and fear about my health and my family.

I'm discouraged. Please help me hang in there, as You did. Rejected, beaten, humiliated, crucified, You did not give up. Grant me the grace to become more like You.

Have mercy on us. I love You.

Mike

Mike, you can count on Me, My grace, and My love. I forgive you, and I AM with you to help you grow in love. Trust Me. I will take care of you and work through you. Slow down and open up to Me and My limitless love for you.

March 15, 1995

Do not be terrified. You are looking for Jesus, Who was crucified? He is risen.

Risen Lord, have mercy on me tonight. I'm stressed out, and I don't know what to eat or drink. I have to fast after midnight for my doctor's appointment. I'm scared I need to do my thing in the morning, but I don't want to get sick. Receive me and heal me. You are my life. I need You— thanks.

I love You.

Mike

I AM with you, the crucified Alpha, Omega, and Almighty One, and I love you. You can count on Me.

March 16, 1995

Are you the Christ, the son of the Blessed One? I AM.

They condemned Him to death.

Lord,

I'm better but still pretty wiped out, by stress and sickness, by lack of sleep and nutrition. I'm feeling lousy, and I'm sick, but I want to get better. Please help me take small steps and not give up.

You are with me. You are our personal God and savior. All praise to You, for what You went through for love of us all. Receive me, broken, sinful, and hoping to grow in my relationship with You. Help me treasure our relationship. You are my friend and are always at my side. I can count on You and lean on You for help.

Thanks. I love You. Have mercy on us.

Love, Mike

March 17, 1995

They crucified Jesus and the robbers. Jesus said, "Father, forgive them, they know not what there are doing."

Lord, I am stressed out. My anorexia is making me constipated, and I'm angry, I am so caught up in myself. I don't want to change. I am sinful. I am pathetic.

Mike. It's ok. It's ok to be angry. Experience it, and then let go of it. It's causing you fear. I love you. You don't need to anything to be loveable in my eyes. You are unique and good. You have problems, and you are sinful, but you are still precious and beautiful.

Thanks. I love You. Have mercy on us.

March 18, 1995

It is finished. Father, into your hands I commend My spirit.

Then, bowing His head, He died.

Mike, I died on the cross for you. I want you. If you want to meet Me, you must die to your selfishness. Dying is painful, but it is necessary for rebirth. You must die to your old self so that I can make my dwelling in you and with you and through you. I offer you life. Believe in my love for you.

Lord, forgive for my sinfulness, I'm useless, yet You love me so much. Thanks. Receive me tonight, stress out over self, health, diet, weight, and family. I place all my hurts, worries, disappointments, and fears in You. Help me to trust in You and to surrender what separates me from You.

Thanks. I love You. Have mercy on us.

March 19, 1995

Gospel. Reform. The barren fig tree gets an extra year.

God's mercy and love are limitless. Our time to respond is limited.

Dear Lord,

I am challenged to reform at this point. My anorexia has led me into a life of seclusion and selfishness. You call me to turn away from my sins and sinfulness and to believe the Good News—that You, Most Holy One, love me, that You suffered for me and died for me, and that You are with me now to help me grow. It's overwhelming. Help me take small steps and be patient.

The fruit tree was given an extra year for You to work with it. Let me to be patient too and make small changes, in eating, in my social life, and in my prayer. With Your help, I can make it. I am changing, slowly, because of You. Thanks.

Receive me with my hopes and fears tonight. I also offer a prayer for my brother. If it be Your will, help him get a new job and a new opportunity in life, and make Your help known to him.

Thanks. I love You. Have mercy on us.

Love, Mike

March 20, 1995

Forgive me for being like Pilate (afraid) and Herod (selfish). Forgive me for letting my fears and my self-preoccupation blind me and stop me from knowing You. They missed out, and I regret that I too have let things come between us.

Help me to let go and surrender. Thanks.

Not My will, but Your will be done, Father.

Mike, you want to know the truth, and the truth will set you free.

Lord, I am stressed tonight. I offer my feelings to You, and I pray, Lord, to be like You, surrendering my life to Your Father's will. Help me come to truly know You by surrendering my will. In knowing You I will know freedom, in You, my loving God and savior.

March 21, 1995

Are You the Christ, the son of the Blessed One? I AM.

Mike, I AM. I AM your personal savior and God. I want you to offer yourself to Me in love. Only then will you find wholeness.

Lord,

Help me fight my anorexia, my fear of weight gain and digestive problems, and my worries about my brother. Receive me and forgive me for not being open to You and for being so distrustful.

Heal and have mercy on me, a sinner. Thanks. I love You.

Mike

March 22, 1995

Don't weep for Me, weep for yourself and your children.

Mike, open up, see Me in others. I am in them, and I long for them to love Me.

Lord, forgive me that I am so caught up in myself that I neglect You. At least the women responded to You. I am too caught up in myself, please help me to love and be loved.

Thanks for Your love for me. I love You. Have mercy on us.

March 23, 1995

Father, grant me the grace to reject sin and accept Your calling me to follow Your son. Thanks for calling my father. Jesus have mercy on me, a sinner. Come, Holy Spirit, come. Glory to You, Most Holy God.

Don't weep for Me, weep for yourself and your children.

Dear Lord,

Broken, exhausted, bleeding, and beaten, You continued to bear the cross for us. You did not get caught up in self-pity and self-preoccupation as I do. You reached out to the women who wept, because they loved You.

Lord, forgive me for not appreciating and focusing on Your pain and Your love. I'm so caught up in my own problems. Forgive me too for being blind to my brothers' and sisters' needs. They call out for love and compassion, and I'm too tired, sick, and busy. Lord, help me to stop focusing on myself and to be open to You and to loving my brothers and sisters. In loving, I'm enriched, for I can come to know You better. And Lord, grant me the spirit of repentance and remorse, the power to be sad and sorry for my sins and for the sinfulness of the hierarchy I'm a part of.

Lord, forgive me

—for being too busy, too sick, and too tired to care and listen.

—for shutting others out.

—for judging, callously and indifferently.

—for my gossip, pride, and ingratitude.

—for the years of lost opportunities to love.

—for hurting those who love me through my selfishness and sickness.

—for the lying, phony image I've created.

—for my selfishness and vanity.

Lord, forgive me. I'm a broken sinner and unable to change on my own. Grant me the grace to become more like You, loving even when I'm hurting, never giving up, taking a step at a time with You.

Lord, help me. Receive my anxiety, fears, and worries about weight and sinfulness. Help me to change. Have mercy on me and on us.

Thanks. I love You.

Love, Mike

Mike, don't be too hard on yourself. I love you, I AM with you, and I AM teaching you and helping you carry your cross. Believe in Me and My love for you—in that lies your strength.

March 24, 1995

The men who were guarding Jesus made fun of Him and beat Him.

Lord,

You were humiliated and beaten for being Yourself and being true to what Your Father called You to do for us. You were Yourself despite the ugly consequences. You could have been a phony, someone who didn't make waves, but You were You, a lover, and this cost You—You could have hidden from life and played it safe and selfishly, but instead You risked being You and accepted the consequences.

Forgive me. I live a lie, creating an image, terrified to be who I am. I am not even sure who that is, he is buried beneath so much garbage. I'm messed up. Help me to get in touch with the real me and let go of the sick image that I maintain to the point of exhaustion, which has hurt me and others. Forgive me for all I have wasted—life, time, opportunities to be Your witness to the world.

I'm overwhelmed by how messed up I am. There seems to be no hope. I am upset and distracted during my time with You. My eating behavior, shutting myself off from others, staying up all night—these are my cross. Thanks for listening to my babbling on.

Love, Mike

Mike, you are doing good work. Hang in there and keep making small changes. I AM your crucified, lover, savior and God. I AM the Almighty. I AM more powerful than your problems. Trust in Me and let go, and together we can win! I love you.

March 24, 1995

They crucified Him.

Mike, I have chosen you out of this world to be Mine. On the cross I suffered for your sins because I love you and want you for Myself. Believe that I forgive you and love you. I AM with you. I offer you Me and a new life.

Lord, receive me, an unworthy sinner, thankful and awed at the sacrifice You made for me. My faith is weak—I am weak—forgive me for not appreciating the great gift You made me, and for not being open to You in my daily life. Help me be open to You and Your saving love. Receive my worries, my fears, and my whole self—I offer me to You. Use me as an instrument of Your love.

Have mercy on us. Thanks. I love You.

Mike

March 25, 1995

They crucified him.

I have chosen you out of this world.

Mike, I want you to be mine, to know Me and My love for you. I know you are sick and sinful and hurting. I call you out of slavery to the world and to your sickness. Let go and be open to Me and My love for you.

Dear Lord,

Receive me tonight, broken, worried about drugs, brothers, and sleep. Help me to accept Your call and to receive You as my lord, savior, lover, and God.

Thanks. I love You. Have mercy on us.

Mike

Dear Friend,

I just wanted You to know how I'm feeling. I haven't accepted my anorexia yet, I'm still fighting and stressed out. I'm very upset and angry, and I gained two pounds (from 99 to 101). What's most upsetting is that all I was doing was drinking milk, which I'd been doing for three weeks with no weight gain. Out of fear of gaining, I've cut back on other areas and intend to do this until I get back to 99. So far, so good, I've lost a little, but I'm stressed out and will probably rethink it. Two weeks of hospital tests screwed up my routine. My system is off. The difficulty is that increased BMS leads to increased movement, and increase in weight leads to stress. It's very upsetting, and I'm angry. If I gain weight I feel doomed, defeated. I like being able to eat M&Ms and not gain.

Help me to hang in there and to hang onto You. I can't make it without You. Receive my anxiety, fear, and anger. Help me keep things in perspective. Help me accept my life, my sickness, and myself, and help me learn to live with my sickness. Help me make positive, healthy, loving changes in my eating, one small step at a time.

Lord, help me be patient with myself and rely on Your grace for this part of my life. Give me what I need to get through the many dark nights. Thanks for healing and answering my prayers.

Have mercy on me, a sinner. I love You.

Mike

March 26, 1995

I will put My spirit in you, that you might live. You will know then that I AM the Lord.

Mike, I AM who AM, I AM God, and I will share the gift of My very self with you. Be open to receiving the gift of My spirit. You will be renewed, transformed, and strengthened, and you will come to know Me and be a witness of My love to your brothers and sisters.

Dear Lord,

Thanks for calling me, accepting me for who I am, and being my savior, God, best friend, and lover. Help me open up to the awesome gift of Yourself—in my powerlessness, I am strong in You. Receive my worries, guilt, sadness, disappointment, hopes, fears, and anxiety—about my health, sleep, eating, weight, and family. Grant me the grace to rejoice in my weakness and become more dependent on You.

Thanks. I love You. Have mercy on us.

Love, Mike

March 27, 1995

They crucified Him.

Mike, slow down and open up to Me in silence.

Dear Lord,

I'm stressed tonight. My stomach hurts, I have constipation and pain, and I'm worried about weight, health, and sleep. Help me, Lord, to turn my life around and work only for You. Help me slow down and listen to You. Help me to pray.

Thanks. I love You. Have mercy on me, a sinner.

Love, Mike

March 28, 1995

They crucified Him.

He saved others, let Him save Himself if He is the messiah of God.

Dear Lord,

Help me enter into Your silence—the silence of the cross, the language and the essence of love. I am too much like the Pharisees. I try to make religion my own thing when it is not my thing at all but a relationship with You. O Most Holy God, help me slow down and stop my obsessive rattling of words and be aware and in awe of You, my God, savior and lover.

Receive me tonight, anxious about food, weight, bathroom, and grant me the grace to open myself up to You and make You my personal lord, savior, king, and lover. Help me to let go of what separates us.

Thanks. I love You. Have mercy on me, a sinner.

Love, Mike

Mike, open up to Me. I AM in you, and I want a covenant relationship with you. I want you to be Mine.

March 29, 1995

Have you no fear of God seeing that we are under the same sentence? This man has done nothing wrong.

Jesus, remember me.

Dear Lord,

I'm too much like the Pharisees—closed to You by pride and thinking I can "earn" health by the mere repetition of words. Help me pray from my heart. Help me to recognize You as the repentant thief did.

You call me to intimacy—thanks. Receive my anxiety tonight about eating and weight. Help me to change.

Thanks. I love You. Have mercy on us.

Love, Mike

Mike, open up to Me. Slow down. Listen I AM with you.

March 30, 1995

Jesus, remember me.

I assure you, this day you will be with Me in paradise.

Mike, you are very hard on yourself. You are human, weak, imperfect, and sinful—and also very loving and very good. You are precious, made in My image, and I love you. Slow down and open up to recognize Me and experience My healing, love, and forgiveness. I want you to be Mine. I value you, and I died for you, that you might share in My life.

Dear Lord,

Thanks for the gift of faith. It is my life. You are my life.

I'm sorry for getting stuck in my own head and not appreciating and recognizing You in my life. Please help me, I'm sick. I'm stressed because I gained one or two pounds. I was angry, but now I'm sad. I'll be ok, though—I know I can count on You.

Receive my desire to change, grow, and love. Help me to relax, pray, and relate to You as my lover. Help me to live simply and be good to myself. Grant me rest, and receive my worries. You will see me through.

Thanks. I love You.

Mike

April 1, 1995

They crucified Him.

Mike, I died. I gave My life so that you might have life. I give you Myself daily. Open up, slow down, and meet Me in this sacrament of now. I want you to be Mine. I AM in love with you. You are precious—be still and know that I AM.

Dear Lord,

I'm exhausted. I fasted all day. I feel sick, stressed, worried, anxious, and tired. Receive me tonight. Thanks for dying for us and giving Yourself to me. Forgive me for not being open, reverent, and thankful, and help me become more like You, my lover. Help me let go and open myself up to know You as my crucified savior and lover.

Thanks. I love You. Have mercy on me.

Love, Mike

April 2, 1995

O My people—oh, Michael.

I will put My spirit in you that you may live. You will then know that I AM the Lord.

I offer You me today. I am stressed out. I stopped losing weight steadily at 102. I'm trying to continue, to make it part of me to lose weight, but life distracts me in every direction. I am depressed and angry. Why can't I get better?

I know I can, but I don't want to keep cutting back, because illness, hospitals and death will hurt my family.

Lord, I am very sick. I need help. Help me, Lord, I need You. You offer me Your love, forgiveness, help, and life—You offer me Your very self. May I be open to the gift of Your spirit, so that I might live a new life in You. But to do that, I must die to my selfish self. Help me, Lord.

Have mercy on us. Thanks. I love You.

April 4, 1995

Lord, I am worn out. Every morning, I sit before You in silence, happy and hopeful to trust You. Thoughts race through my mind, though, distractions, that need to be dealt with. I am sick, very sick, and twisted.

It seems that I lost it. From 100 to 102. I feel fat, bloated, constipated, my bladder is full. It's a living hell for me. I'm hungry all day, drinking all night, then up going to the bathroom. I am exhausted, I am overwhelmed, I need help. But I fear change.

I know You want me to face my illness and deal with it. I need to work with the trust You have given me to help me. Yet I resist, Lord. I'm powerless and helpless.

I offer You my pain and sorrow and sickness today, and I ask for the grace to be open to You and Your love, that I myself may begin to love. Only then will I have life.

Lord, I am angry because my way has not worked, but I am scared to let go and change. Please help me to surrender. You surrendered Your life and will on the cross, and You took on the pain and sin of all humankind. I know that I too must surrender and die to myself. Forgive me for being so resistant and selfish. Grant me the grace to let go.

Thanks. Have mercy on us. I love You.

Mike, open up to meet me, one step at a time. Be patient. I AM with you, and I will help you get through your suffering.

April 5, 1995

They took Jesus and led Him away bearing the cross for Himself.

Mike, hang in there. I AM with you. Don't be afraid—pain leads to growth in My love.

Lord, You were broken, whipped, spit on, scourged, and crowned with thorns, and then You were sent to be crucified. Taunted and humiliated, You picked up Your cross and struggled to Golgotha. Exhausted, beaten, bleeding, and hurting, You carried it for us one step at a time.

It was "our weaknesses that He carried"; it was "our sufferings He endured."

You took our broken, sinful nature on Your shoulders and were "pierced for our sins." Lord, in caring Your cross You showed how persistent, determined and unwavering Your love is for me. You didn't quit because You loved Your Father and You loved us. Help me to carry my cross. I won't make it on my own, Lord. I'm too messed up, sinful, and weak.

Help me accept my anorexia. I've been angry lately, and I seem to be gaining weight. I don't want to, but I'm famished, and I have to keep eating. Maybe I haven't gained—maybe my system is out of whack and I'm not removing waste from my body regularly as I did when I weighed two or three pounds less.

I know that's crazy, but it's where my head is right now. I'm sick and selfish because I don't want to let go of this, I've relied on it to feel good for so long. Forgive me for being resistant to change. I'm scared, tired, depressed, and angry, yet I'm hopeful. I'm slowly progressing. Help me carry this, my cross, my way to You.

April 6, 1995

That bread I will give you is My flesh for the life of the world. Let Me feed and nourish you, live with and through you.

Mike, I AM with you. I will give you what you need to make it. I give you Me. Open yourself up to a personal relationship with Me. You will find what you long for.

Dear Lord,

Receive me. Thanks for giving me a new start. I'm still struggling with anorexia yet hopeful. It's ok that I gained; I'll try to lose a little by cutting back. Yeah, I'm sick but I'm working on getting better. I've had a small setback, and I'm only gaining slowly. Weight gain upsets me, but it's ok. I'm not going to cut way back.

I offer my struggles and thank You for the opportunity to become dependent on You. I need You. Help me to open up to Your call to a personal relationship.

My life, savior, lord, and God—Thanks. I love You.

Mike

April 7, 1995

They crucified Him.

Mike, I love you and I AM with you. Believe and listen.

Lord,

I'm on vacation, thanks. I'm also working at cutting back—I have to do it to feel good. Help me accept myself and open up to You: You are my only hope, You are my life, and I offer You this week. Help to open up to Your love and develop a personal relationship with You, and help me show Your love to those I spend time with. Thanks for the gift of Yourself and my life.

Have mercy on us. Thanks. I love You.

Love, Mike

April 8, 1995

Don't be afraid of anything. I AM with you. —Psalms 23

I don't condemn you. —John 8

Mike, I don't condemn you. I forgive you. I love you for who you are. Believe, and share, and don't be afraid—I AM with you.

Lord, receive me tonight. Thanks for opening me up to You. Thanks for giving Yourself up for me. I'm upset tonight—weight, diet, constipation, bleeding—so please help me trust in Your love and not be afraid.

Have mercy on us. Thanks. I love You.

Dear Lord,

Receive me today. My vacation is starting, and I'm sick as a dog—broken, scared, angry, depressed, anorexic—I got sick again last night—and hungry. I gained weight again. 103! Drank too much juice. Another failure. I want to cry. Forgive me, Lord, for being so mixed up, so broken and sinful, I feel like a disappointment—to You, to my family, to the world I live in, because I'm so messed up.

Lord, forgive me—help me. I love You, I need You, I want to know You more. Despite my pain I find comfort in You. You are my savior, my crucified lord, my lover, and my God. Be with me and help me to love. Help me make this vacation a time of loving. I'm broken, but maybe that's ok. Maybe You can use a misfit like me.

Thanks for accepting me as I am, in good and bad, in high and low, in sickness and pain, in hope and joy. Have mercy on us.

I love You.

April 9, 1995, Palm Sunday

Mike, I love you and want you to be Mine. I want you to know Me and to know how precious you are to Me.

Lord, I am not worthy. I am a sinner. It's Holy Week, when You died for me.

Lord, I am poor, weak, and sinful, and I do not deserve what You have given me, I am so caught up in selfish concerns. Please forgive me for being such a poor servant. That is the beauty and awesomeness of Your passion, death, and resurrection—that You reach out to me in love and give me grace and the desire for You, though I could never be worthy of it in my broken sinfulness. I am awed that You came to save me, at the purity of Your gift, that my God would do so much for me.

Thanks for calling a broken sinner in faith to know You. Help me treasure this gift and Your call in my poverty, for I am extremely rich. I've been blessed with faith, hope, and love. Help me treasure our relationship above all else and show Your love to my brothers and sisters Help me this week to die to myself, and forgive me for self-pity, and vanity over my image and diet. Forgive me, Lord, and help me change.

Thanks. I love You. Have mercy on us all.

April 10, 1995

"Father, into your hands I commend my spirit." And bowing his head he died.

Clearly this was an innocent man.

Lord, You died for us all. You gave all You had. You suffered, bled, and were suffocated till You were unable to continue.

Lord, I come before You a sinner, broken and messed up, because I hear You calling me in my heart. Lord, forgive me for my prayer. It is routine, so mechanical and compulsive. Grant me the grace to relate to You as my best friend, brother, and lover—as a person, one who is truly human and truly divine—and as an "innocent man." You suffered as the Paschal Lamb to take away our sins. I'm sorry for being so caught up in myself. I've wasted a lot, but please help me give this week, of myself and my time, to You and others. Help me too to receive. I'm so proud and very closed—bless me with thankfulness and openness.

I love You. Have mercy on us.

Love, Mike

Dear Lord,

Help me see the dignity of taking up my cross to follow You this week. I offer my suffering, nothing in comparison to Yours or that of so many others, but all I have to give right now.

I'm stressed, worried, depressed, and angered by my sickness and not being able to lose weight the way I want to. And I'm so sick—physically exhausted, sleeping and eating poorly, suffering bodily problems. And mostly it is my own self that I am hurting—me whom You died for. Forgive me.

Although I'm sinful, help me see what value I do have, as a child of broken humanity yet one made in Your likeness. Thanks for the gift of myself and my life—*our* life. Help me honor the gift of being someone You created. May I reverence and respect the lives of all human beings including myself. You paid and incredible price for each of us. Thanks.

I love You. Have mercy on us.

Love, Mike

Mike, it's ok. Be less hard on yourself. I love you very much, and because I became one of you and knew your pain, it's ok. I AM with you and love you very much. You are a special friend— still sick and hurting and sinful, yet still beautiful and loveable. I delight in your desire to be close to Me. Do it—carry your cross one step at a time. I AM with you and will help you make it.

April 11, 1995

Who is it you are looking for?

I AM He. Let the other men go.

Lord, You are the Lamb of God who takes away our sins. You became a substitute, facing in Your passion and death the consequences of my own sins and the sins of all people, evils that lead to pain and death. You took our pain because You love us, and we have no hope without You. You let me off the hook because You loved me, to save me from my sinfulness. Most Holy Son of God, You were courageous and loving despite Your fear and anxiety. You didn't give up but kept loving. I give up so often, but You forgave me. Grant me the grace to be open to the gift of salvation.

You died so that might gain friendship with God and with my brothers and sisters. Forgive me for not sharing this gift above all else. With my anorexia, I've let my selfishness, vanity, and pride become an obsession that blocks me from a deeper relationship with You. You took my sin and brokenness so that I might be healed and saved. I offer You me, with my hurt, stress, weight gain, exhaustion, nervousness, and poor health. I am angry that my way is not helping anymore. I am sad that I am messed up. Receive me, Lord, as a broken sinner who wants to repent and change and become Your friend.

I am so resistant to letting go. Chris told me to be more patient, that letting go is a praise at dying to oneself and a time to be reborn into a holy relationship with You, most Holy God.

Thanks. I love You. Have mercy on us.

Mike

Mike, as a true human I can identify with your pain. Trust in me. Repenting and becoming a lover will not be easy, but I AM with you each step of the way and will give you what you need.

April 12, 1995

Am I not to drink the cup the Father has given me?

"Are you not one of the man's followers?" "Not I."

Although you rejected me, I will not reject you.

Following Me involves sacrificing your way, leaving your comfort zone, to take the risk of loving. This is my will for you: to grow. You can do this only if you die to your selfish self, risk love, and give yourself to Me and others. I want you to be My lover and a Lover for Me.

Lord,

In fear and selfishness, I often fail to push myself outside my safety zone. Grant me the grace to take loving risks and be Your disciple, not simply a bystander. Today, I began growing up. U am hopeful though still resistant to change, and I feel good. Thanks for the good sleep and healing. My body is getting better, and I am realizing that I want to risk myself to love. Isolation and selfishness are not Your way for me—You call me to the way of love.

Thanks; grant me the grace to love. Have mercy on us all. I love You.

Mike

Lord,

Stressed—weight gain—angry—sad.

I need You.

Mike

Mike, I am with you, I am all you need, in the Eucharist.

Take this and eat—this is My Body which will be given up for you.

I know you cannot make it on your own. I want to give My life and My love to you so that you can live. Open up, let go, and become dependent on Me for your life.

Lord,

I got sick today—sick, sick, sick, I binged, I took laxatives, I'm broken. Help me get through this and begin again. Thanks. I love You,

Mike

April 14, 1995, Good Friday

They crucified Him

"Father, forgive them"

Mike, I died to save you from sin and evil. I died for you because I love you and want you to have a personal relationship with Me. I AM your God, savior, lover and friend.

Lord,

I need a friend right now. Sitting alone in my sickness, I binged last night, missed Mass, purged with Ex-Lax, and took pain pills to knock me out because I didn't want to feel bad today. I'm numb and in shock. It's been maybe three years since I last got sick, although realistically I'm sick even today, filling up on liquids, depending on juice to get regular sleep, exhausted and depressed. That's a normal day for me. I should be mediating on Your passion and love, but I am too sick. Forgive me.

I'm unworthy and can never be worthy of Your love. Calvary was an undeserved gift for all mankind. Thank You, Lord. In my brokenness, You have always been there—through my ups and downs over many years, You have never abandoned me but always loved, forgiven, and accepted me. Thanks. I offer You my life and suffering today—I cannot make it in this world on my own. Help me to live and depend on You as I must. Thanks.

Have mercy on me and us all. I love You.

Mike

April 15, 1995, Holy Saturday

Oh my people, I will open your graves and have you rise. —Ezekiel 37

Mike, hope in Me. I will get you through your days of suffering and sickness.

Lord, I got sick on Thursday, binged and purged, knock myself out with pills, and was sick all Friday and into today. I'm devastated, numb, angry, sad, and disappointed in myself. I feel dead, broken, helpless, unsure even what I should even eat today. I am lost. This is the sickest I have ever been. My body, aged from anorexia, cannot take this stress. My insides are messed up, and I am terrified. Lord, I don't know what to do or how to live—I need You. Without You I am lost. I long for You, Lord. You are my only hope. Help me to trust, to want, to listen, and to depend on You. Thanks for hearing and answering my prayers. I love You. Have mercy on us.

April 16, 1995, Easter Sunday

Don't be terrified. You are looking for Jesus, who was crucified. He is risen. He is not here.

Mike, don't be afraid. I AM your crucified savior and lord. I AM risen and I AM with you to share My life with you. Believe in Me—be and live in Me.

Alleluia! Praise to You, Risen Lord, receive me today. Help me to know You as my personal savior and lord. Save me from my sinfulness and sickness, and help me to share the Good News of Your love with my brothers and sisters.

Thanks. I love You. Have mercy on us all.

April 17, 1995

Peace be with you, Mike. Receive me as your savior and know my love for you, which is peace. Be fearful and in awe, yet take refuge in me, for I will save you.

Risen Lord, receive me tonight. I am broken by weight gain and stressed out from dieting—unsuccessfully. I feel guilty and angry with myself for failing.

I have fully accepted You as my savior and the lord of my life. Forgive me, Risen Lord, for being closed. Help me to be open in awe and fear and to receive You into my heart as my personal God, savior, and lover.

Do not be terrified. You are looking for Jesus, who was crucified. He has been raised up. He is not here.

Mike, believe in Me and My love for you.

Lord, receive me today. I'm stressed out again. Just back to work after my vacation and already getting really sick. I'm scared and angry about my weight gain, and my lack of control, and I've been knocked off my high horse. I am really sick, and I'm fighting to lose, and I'm helpless and hopeless without You and others. I'm discouraged, my whole life is a mess, and I can't make it on my own. Yet You died for me, and as my risen lord and savior You call me to accept You and develop a loving personal relationship with You. Help me, please, and grant me the grace to respond to Your call and let go of what separates me from You. Help me to trust that You will take care of me. Help me to set my heart on You, Your will, and Your kingdom. Nothing else is important.

Thanks. Have mercy on me, a helpless sinner. I love You

Mike

April 18, 1995

Peace

Happy are those that take refuge in me.

Mike, find forgiveness, peace, healing, and love in calling on Me today.

Lord,

I'm sick again. I lost it. I'm angry, sad, and disappointed again at my weight gain and loss of control. My life is a mess, and I feel powerless and broken. My savior, I offer You me this day and ask You to grant me the grace of Your forgiveness and peace. Help me to take refuge in You and call on You in reverence each step of the way. Thanks for showing me how much I need You. Help me to trust You and pray constantly. You are my only hope.

Thanks. I love You. Have mercy on us.

Mike

Mike, when you called on me, I answered. I AM your God and your personal savior, crucified and risen. Don't be afraid. I offer you My peace, forgiveness, and help. I offer you life and love. Depend on Me in your sickness, for I AM your strength in your weakness.

Lord,

Thanks. I have been sick since last night. I can't make it on my own, but I'm beginning to believe in Your love for me and Your power to save me when I call. Thanks to my trust in You, I am finding strength, hope, peace, and love.

Thanks. Have mercy on us. I love You.

Mike

April 19, 1995

Mike, When you call to Me, I will answer and save you. Be at peace and don't be afraid. Depend on Me.

Lord, thanks. You are My strength and My savior. All praise to You, o Risen Christ—with You I have life. Help me to begin anew in dependence on You. Thanks. I love You. Have mercy on me, a sinner.

April 20, 1995

At the sight of Him, the Risen Lord, those who doubted fell down in homage.

Full authority has been given to me, both in Heaven and on Earth. Go therefore and make disciples, and know that I AM with you always

Mike, I want to be your savior and friend, and I want you to be Mine and to share with others the good news of your life with Me.

Lord,

Receive me tonight. I've been wiped out for the past week, physically, emotionally, and spiritually. I've been sick twice. I'm thankful and hopeful tonight, though. I can't make it on my own, my way won't work—I'm still frustrated and struggling with weight gain. Help me to accept myself, and thanks for teaching me how much I need You and for giving me the grace I need to get back on track and make it through every day. Help me remember to call on You often, knowing that You are with me always and want to be my savior, and that You will answer me when I call out in reverence. In my weakness, Your power is revealed. Help me develop a truly personal relationship with You, O Most Holy and loving Risen Savior.

Thanks. Have mercy on me. I love You.

Love, Mike

April 21, 1995

They crucified Him.

I AM with you always, I AM in you, and I will help you when you call on Me. I love you very much. I want to be your savior and I want you to be Mine.

Dear Lord,

I'm stressed out and angry trying to handle it. Help me. Why did I have to gain all this weight, from 99 to 106 now. I've barely been eating any more. I'd hoped that I could increase my intake and not gain, maybe even continue to lose, but I guess my metabolism is too low. And I've "gained" even more due to increased liquids and fiber—it's not real gain but it shows on the scales. It's upsetting—if it means gaining this much, I don't want to eat better. I'm disappointed and disgusted, and I can't wear the clothes I want to.

I want to get control again. I lost it on vacation, and again this week, but now on day 4 I'm finding that You will give me the strength to not get sick, and I'm feeling better, hopeful and thankful. Now I need to decrease my intake and liquids so that my butt can heal and I can sleep. Help me continue to change and eat healthy. I want to cut back and lose, and to build on that so I feel safe and in control. I believe I can do this, and I feel better taking it one step at a time, seeing that I'm making it.

Today was the first day in two weeks that I've not had lots of gas and pain. I'm getting better. Thanks. I know I messed up a lot, but I'm making progress, I'm making healthy choices that I can build on—help me to hang in there and become more dependent on You. Help me to be free and open to my relationship with You

Thanks. Have mercy on me, I love You.

Love, Mike

April 23, 1995, Emmaus

We were hoping that he would be the one who would set Israel free.

Mike, I AM your crucified and risen lord, God, savior, and lover. I died to set you and all people free from sin and evil. I want you to be free of sins and evil, and to hope and trust and believe in Me. Spend time with Me, listening, as the disciples on the road did, and I will reveal Myself to

you and you will know freedom, wholeness, and love.

Lord, thanks for dying for me and forgiving me. Thanks for giving Your life for me. Help me to open up and receive You as my risen lord, God, savior, and lover. I want to know You—help me to listen. Receive me tonight, a broken sinner hoping to be freed from my sins and brokenness by You, O Holy God. Help me.

Look at My hands and My feet, it is really I. Touch Me.

Rejoice, Mike, for I AM truly and really with you. I love you and I AM here for you.

Praise to You, Holy Savior. Thanks.

April 24, 1995, After Emmaus

Mike. Peace—let go of the thoughts that disturb you turn them over to Me. Look at My wounded hands and feet—I defeated your weakness, and sin. I died and now I am alive, risen, and I offer you Me and My risen life. Open up and rejoice, and let Me be your savior and lover.

Risen Lord,

Thanks. Receive me tonight in my brokenness. Grant me the grace to accept You into my heart as my personal savior. Thanks. I love You. Have mercy on us.

Love, Mike

Mike. Peace—don't be disturbed. Turn your life and your worries over to Me. Look at My hands and feet—I defeated evil and died for you, and now I AM with you. It is I. Trust Me. Reach out and touch Me. Be still and come to know Me.

Lord, receive me, broken and needy. Let me trust You and give You myself in love. Help me to trust, to let go, to be still and open to touch and experience, O Holy Crucified Risen Savior. Thanks. I love You.

Peace. Do not be disturbed. Look at My hands and feet. It is really Me. Touch Me.

Lord, I am so disturbed by worries and cares. Help me accept my sickness and my simple lifestyle, and let me continue to work with the people You have given me to help. I'm scared yet hopeful—help me to trust and surrender to You. You are my savior and my hope. Forgive me for still resisting and for not wanting to deal with those You have put in my life to help me.

Thanks. I love You.

Love Mike,

April 25, 1995

Touch Me. I AM with you.

Lord,

I want to touch and come to know You more. I'm discouraged, worried, and stressed out about my eating problem. My thoughts are sick and broken. I want to develop a personal relationship with You, Lord Jesus. Have mercy on me, a broken sinner.

Thanks. I offer You my love.

Mike

April 26, 1995

Recall that everything written about me had to be fulfilled. He open their minds to the understanding of scripture.

Mike, I AM your reconciliation. I offer you a new life, lost by your sins and won back by My sacrifice and love for you. I want you and love you very much.

Lord, open my mind to You and receive my worries. Have mercy on me. Thanks. I love You.

Mike

April 28, 1995

He opened their minds to the understanding of scriptures.

Mike, in your brokenness you can be open to Me. Open up. I AM here for you, and I AM with you. I AM your strength.

Lord, I'm wiped out. I'm exhausted and angry over my health. I want time off, but my boss says no can do. Forgive me. She's only human too, and my tiredness is my own fault.

Lord, I need to change and I want Your help. Help me to open up. Teach me, and grant me the gift of humility, openness, and reverence. Lord, grant me the gift of life in You. Thanks.

Love, Mike.

April 29, 1995

Worship Me in fear. I will protect you. I AM the joy of those who love My Name.

They crucified Him.

Lord, grant me the grace to slow down and be in awe of Your presence. So often I am in a rush, going through my prayers mechanically and preoccupied with my own worries. Forgive me for my lack of reverence. Thanks for speaking to me and being present. I know You on a personal basis, as my friend, savior, lover, and God, and I must let go and trust that You will protect me. I love Your Holy Name, O Most Glorious Lord, my God. Praise to You.

Help me to keep my life in perspective. I am broken, yes, emotionally, physically, and spiritually, yet with You and by You I am being reborn. You are helping me to be patient and helping me to know You and Your love for my brothers and sisters in this world. Receive me, my hopes and fears and worries.

Have mercy on us. Thanks. I love You

April 30, 1995

Why are you weeping? Who is it you are looking for? I AM ascending to My Father and your Father, to My God and to your God.

Mike, like Mary Magdalene you weep, mourn, and look, yet fail to see me. You cannot "find Me"; I reveal myself to you. My revelation is a pure gift to be accepted in faith. Let go and believe and trust. I AM the way to your heavenly father, God. I AM the bridge. In Me you can find what you need in your brokenness. Continue to worship Me in fear, calling on Me, and I will reveal Myself to you.

Lord,

Tonight I am hurting. I am stressed out about my eating problem and from knowing I have not surrendered my life and will to You. Receive me in my brokenness and grant me the grace to surrender to You and Your love for me. Thanks for the life-saving gift of faith. Help me to be open to meeting You.

Love, Mike

May 3, 1995

Peace.

He showed them His hand and side.

As the Father has sent Me, so I send you.

He breathes on them. Receive the Holy Spirit.

Mike, know that I love you very much and call you to unity to My Father's love. I know you cannot make it without us. Be open and receive the Holy Spirit, who will empower you.

Worship Me in fear and I'll protect you. I AM the joy of those who love My Name. Call on Me often. I AM with you, and I love you.

Lord,

Thanks for getting me through a rough and painful day. I called on You and You answered me.

My life is out of control—I'm sick and hurting and sinful. But I offer You myself and my worries. Help me to let go and to trust and give my life over to Your guidance. Grant me the grace I need to be a loving servant. Thanks for being my savior, and for the awesome gift of Your life and Yourself.

Have mercy on me. I love You.

Love, Mike

May 4, 1995

Mike. Peace. See My hands and My side. I died for you, and I love you. I AM with you, your risen crucified savior, God, and lover, and I send you to love as My Father sent me. You can do nothing on you own. Be open to the gift of the comforter, the Holy Spirit. He will give you the strength you need to face your brokenness and the strength you need to go forth and be a witness.

Dear Lord,

Leceive me tonight, broken and scared. My sickness and my sin are too much for me to handle. My life is out of control. I thought I lost it last night. I was sick as a dog in my brokenness and pain. Help me to rely more on You.

I am angry. I gained four pounds, and I'm now at 104. I'm afraid I lost control. I want to look thin and feel good. I used to weigh 110. Ten years ago I was 127 and already really thin. I know I am sick. I'll probably be content and feel good if I can lose weight. But when I am losing, I am not helping myself, and I am exhausted. Help me to change.

Linda and her family pointed out that I need to change. I am a broken person. I was hurt badly as a young child, and again as a teen. I am broken and hurt, sick, ugly, and sinful, yet I am loveable. I am not totally bad. Deep inside is the me whom You died for and called me to become. I still have to go through a lot of pain to get to the real me, though. Help me. My life and my family are Your gifts, praised and saved. Help me value the gift of me whom You died to save.

Thank You. I love You. Have mercy on me.

Love, Mike

Peace be with you. See My hands and My side. I love you, and I AM with you. Worship Me in fear, call on Me often, and I'll protect and save you. Find life and joy in Me, for I AM the joy of those who love My Name.

Dear Lord,

What a night. I'm full of anxiety, panic, and stress, and I almost binged, overwhelmed by what I need to do. I have to go back to work on my life, to work through the hurt, humiliation, shame, and guilt, and begin to feel what I never allow myself to feel. I need to get in touch with frightening things and let myself experience them. I need to change, even though change terrifies me—I like my fish-bowl life too much, and the security it offers. I'm angry and scared. I don't want to go through this yet, but I believe You want me to do this and to begin to love myself and others as You love me.

Risen Lord, I can't make it without You, like the disciples. I am locked behind walls of fear. You showed them Your risen life—May I too be open to Your love and to the joy of that new life. Forgive me my sins, and receive me broken but at peace, for I know I am powerless. In my brokenness, I'm learning my need for You. I not only need You, I want You in my life. Please guide me.

Thanks for revealing Yourself and offering me the help I need to grow. Receive my worries about change, and help me to trust in You one moment at a time. Thanks for loving me so very much.

Have mercy on me, a sinner. I love You.

Love, Mike

May 5, 1995

They crucified Him.

Father, forgive them.

Worship me in fear.

Lord,

Forgive me for not making time for You, for being caught up in me and my sickness. Forgive me, and help me to worship You in fear and get to know You. Your love and forgiveness for me are limitless.

Thanks. I love You. Have mercy on us.

Love, Mike

May 6, 1995

Mike, open up. Listen and trust. I AM your God, crucified savior, best friend, and lover. Call on Me. I am with you to help you. I give Myself to you daily. Listen, open up, trust, and love.

Receive me tonight, Lord, in my worries and hopes. Jesus Christ, Son of God, have mercy on me, a sinner. Thanks. I love You.

May 7, 1995

See my wounded hands and side—Do not pursue your unbelief, but believe—Blest are they who have not seen and believe.

Worship me in fear. Call on me often. I will protect you.

Mike, you are blessed with the gift of faith, and you must nurture it, by praying, by calling on Me often and love. Learn to trust. I will get you through the week at work. I AM your savior.

Lord, receive me tonight. Thanks for the awesome, life-giving gift of faith and for being present and speaking to me. Help me to rely on You more. I worry about the changes, yet I know I must face them, so give me the grace I need to make it.

Thanks. Have mercy on me a sinner. I love You.

Mike

May 8, 1995

Don't persist in your unbelief, but believe.

My lord and my God.

Mike, I AM your crucified and risen lord and God and savior. I AM with you to help you and protect you. Trust Me and love Me.

Lord, thanks. I'm feeling good and rested. Receive me tonight. Out of stress, I indulged in pastry and food. I feel fat because I'm at 104 and not 100. I'm sick, yes, and struggling, yes, but I'm hopeful because You are giving me what I need. Help me to focus on what is truly important— You, my lord and God. You are life. I am blessed and called to be in a covenant relationship with You. How awesome it is. Thanks for blessing me with faith, the greatest treasure. Help me to worship You in fear, to call on You often, and to listen and trust.

May 9, 1995

Mike, believe that I AM the Messiah, the Son of God. Through faith in Me, you can have life in My Name. Worship Me in fear and call on Me often.

Lord, receive me tonight, stressed out at weight gain that I can't seem to lose. I am angry and feel like a failure, and I miss the attention and pity my weight loss got me. I am so selfish, so stressed, out and so afraid. At Big G's ordination party, I was caught up in it. I'm sick, broken, selfish, and sinful. Forgive me, Lord, for putting this vanity above others. You have given me faith, the greatest gift I could receive, and I don't deserve it. You have blessed me, and despite the living hell of my anorexia, I have never given up my faith. It is a pure gift You gave that sustains me, and I could lose it. I truly have life in Your name, Most Holy One. Without You, I am nothing. Help me hear, through the pain, how You call me to depend on You. Grant me the grace to accept You in my heart as my personal lord, savior, lover, and God. Help me trust in You, Holy Friend.

Thanks. I love You. Have mercy on me, a sinner.

Love, Mike

May 10, 1995

Mike, believe in Me. I AM your messiah and God, and your faith in Me is My gift. Treasure it, find life in Me, and call on Me in fear. I AM here now and will always be available to help you.

Lord, receive me. Thanks for the faith, for the healing. I was sick this morning, and You got me through it. Receive my stress and worries about health, weight, employment, and the family get-together. I'm tired and frustrated, and I can't seem to lose weight. I have so many demands on my time, guilt, resentment, and exhaustion from pushing myself. Help me find or make time to be relaxed with myself and You.

Thanks again. I love You. Have mercy on me, a sinner

Love, Mike

May 11, 1995

Mike, believe in Me. I AM with you, your messiah and lord. I AM your God. Open up to Me and My love for you.

O Lord, our God, how glorious is Your most holy name through all the earth. Grant me the grace to accept You as my savior, lover, and God, and to praise You. Thanks for healing my pain, for my growth and healing and dependence on You. Help me to accept myself, and my weight gain, and help me become a loving person and rely on You. Receive my worries tonight, about health, weight, eating, working, and partying. Grant me the grace to continue and to depend on You.

Thanks. Have mercy on me. I love You.

Love, Mike

May 12, 1995

Mike, don't let your heart be troubled. Have faith in God, have faith in Me. Worship Me in fear. I will protect you, call on Me often. I AM the joy for those who love Me Name. I AM with you, Mike, and I died for you. I love you and want you to be Mine. Believe and trust.

My loving Lord, receive me tonight, thankful. I have had a beautiful day off. Thanks for the precious gift of life and faith. Thanks for speaking to me and giving Yourself to me and being with me. Thanks for the peace of mind I feel, and thanks for Your gift of Yourself on the cross.

Tonight I feel stress—about food, fat, sleep, being up early, using the bathroom, partying, food, and relatives—stress and exhaustion, fear and anger. I am sick, broken, and sinful, but I am slowly getting better physically, emotionally, and spiritually. Grant me the grace to accept You as my savior, lord, lover, and God, and to call on You often. You are with me. Help me to listen and be an instrument of Your love to my brothers and sisters.

Thanks. I love You. Have mercy on us.

Love Mike

I have heard you cry, Mike. I have rescued you. Call on me. Do you love Me? Feed my sheep.

Lord,

Thanks. I called on You in my brokenness, and You answered. You gave me the grace to make it and to be loved, and to love those brothers and sisters who shared in my father's day.

Thanks. I love You. Have mercy on us.

Love, Mike

May 14, 1995

How does this concern you? Your business is to follow Me.

Lord, accept me tonight, broken and sinful yet hopeful. I give You my worries, fears, anger, jealousy, and vanity. Help me to let go and follow You. How scary is Your call. Grant me the grace to respond, worshiping You in awe and love, loving as Your love.

Thanks. Have mercy on me. I love You.

Love Mike

Follow Me. I see your misery, your sorrow. Let me take your pain in My hands. Depend on Me, for I AM your helper. I hear and answer your cry for help . Call on Me.

Have mercy on me Lord. I thank You.

Love Mike.

May 15, 1995

Follow Me.

Lord, I am stressed out today—upset, fighting, and angry. My eating plan didn't pay off, and I'm frustrated. I wanted to lose weight. I'm really struggling and worn out by thinking about how can I improve my nutrition and still lose weight. It's upsetting. I fear losing control, and my butt's acting up. I'm scared too.

Help me to follow You, to seek You and Your Father's way first and only then address my eating issues, trusting that You will guide me. Forgive me for losing track of what is really important. I'm sick, but I'm looking to get better. Help me.

Have mercy on me. Thanks again. I love You.

Love, Mike

May 16, 1995

Mike, as I love you so must you love your brothers—unconditionally, limitlessly, uniquely, and totally. This is how you intercede for me in the world. This is my call: I call you to love your brothers. This is your vocation.

Lord,

Thanks for speaking and being present to me. Thanks for the hope and glory and Your personal call. I am messed up. I have anxiety tonight. Grant me the gift of Your Spirit so that I may love. Thanks. Have mercy on me. I love You.

Love, Mike

Mike, I know you are exhausted and in pain. Take refuge in Me and My love. I will empower you through My Spirit to love and be My witness to the world.

O Glorious Savior, God, thanks.

All praise to You. In You, I have life, hope, security, peace, and wholeness. Receive me, broken, hurting, and sinful. Forgive me for anger at others, and at myself for beating up on myself. Grant me the gift of faith, and through Your Spirit lead me to dwell in You and in Your Father's love, and to share that love.

Have mercy on me. Thanks. I love You.

Love, Mike

They crucified Him.

Mike, I AM with and in you. I AM your refuge. Find peace, strength, and healing in Me. I died for you. I AM your crucified Savior, and I want you.

Lord,

Thanks. forgive me for my selfishness and sinfulness. Heal my brokenness and receive me today, sick, anxiety, worried, exhausted.

I love You. Have mercy on me, thanks.

Love, Mike

May 18, 1995

Mike, take refuge in Me. I will protect you and give you the grace you need. Work hard and be gentle with yourself. I love you because you are you and I know you.

Lord,

Receive me tonight, sick, tired, and exhausted—physically, spiritually, and emotionally. Forgive me for doing unloving things today, and grant healing to anyone I have hurt. Grant me the grace to be thankful and rejoice in my brokenness, for the opportunity it offers me to increase my dependency on You. Help me with my life.

Have mercy on me. Thanks. I love You.

Love, Mike

May 20, 1995

They crucified Him. Father, forgive them.

Mike, I forgive you. Believe, and know My love. I long for you to open up and trust Me and let Me love you. You are precious to Me, and I want you to be Mine.

Lord,

Thanks. My faith in Your love and forgiveness in receiving me, broken, a sinner, anxious, worried, pet hopeful.

Thanks. I love You. Have mercy on us and on me, a sinner.

Love, Mike

May 21, 1995

Don't worry, Mike. Believe in God and in Me. I AM with and in you. Call on Me, in fear and love, for I want to be with you and I want you to be with Me. I AM the way, truth, and life for you and all people.

Lord,

Receive me tonight, stressed about food, weight, guilt over Alice, health, sleep, and family. I am broken and sinful, and offer myself to You. Thanks for increasing my faith in You. Your love and Your forgiveness help me to let go and give myself to You, and in You I am strong and can face the challenges of living.

Thanks. I love You. Have mercy on me, a sinner.

Love, Mike

I AM the Way, Truth, and Life

Mike, look at the crucifix. The cross is your way to Me. Accept it as I did, for it is the way to overcome your brokenness and sin. It is the way to the Father in Me, the sacrificial love with the gift of the Spirit.

Look again, it is the truth. Mike, I AM who AM, your Holy God, who loves you infinitely, totally, uniquely, and unconditionally, and I forgive you.

Receive and see Me on the cross—it is life. I want you to give Me yourself, to be mine and to be in Me, and for ME to be in you, in union, in communion, in the Eucharist, in Food. I want a personal love relationship with you, whom I have called to be My lover.

Lord,

All praise and thanks to You. Grant me the grace to accept and embrace Your call. Self-sacrificing love is the holy way to union with You and my brothers and sisters. Receive me tonight, thankful, and have mercy on me, a sinner. I love You.

Love, Mike

May 23, 1995

Anything you ask in My name, I will do, so as to glorify the Father in the Son.

Lord,

Help me pray in Your name, as You did, glorifying the Father, You, and the Holy Spirit to live in me, and through me to be given glory. Receive me tonight, exhausted. Thanks.

I love You. Have mercy on me, a sinner.

Love, Mike

May 24, 1995

Don't let your heart be troubled. Have faith in God and in Me. I want to be with you and you to be with Me. I AM the Way and the Truth and the Life, your crucified lover and God. Worship Me in fear, call on Me often, and whatever you ask for in My name I will do to glorify My Father.

Lord, receive me.

I slept well for five hours, but it's 3:30 now and I can't get back to sleep. I'm too rested and too stressed, and I'm struggling with my feelings about my eating problem. I'm still angry that I can't seem to lose weight. I'm stuck at 105, and I feel fat. I've starved myself, but I see no progress, and I fear eating and gaining. I'm angry and disappointed. I have insomnia, being up all night and exhausted all day, worrying about the trip to New Jersey. I feel bad, my energy is low, and I'm psychologically down as if I were a heroin junkie. Maybe I am a junkie, seeking a fix to my brokenness in a sick way. I am doing something bad and sinful, and it causes me guilt because it hurts others and it hurts me. I want to take a long vacation, to just get away and sleep a lot, and just *be*. It hurts, to struggle day and night, and takes away my quiet time.

I'm broken, and I know that if I surrender as You did, giving Yourself up to the Father for us all on the cross, I would be responding to Your call. Yet I resist. I'm so selfish, sinful, and sick. Forgive me, Lord.

Have mercy on me, a sick and sinful man. Thanks. I love You.

Mike

Mike, anything you ask in My name I will do. If you love me and help my Samaritans, I will ask My Father and He will send you another Paraclete, the Spirit of Truth.

Lord, receive me tonight, sick, exhausted, worried, and sinful, in poor health and broken. Yet tonight I have hope. Grant me the grace to pray in Your most holy name, seeking to do all for Your Father's glory. Grant me the gift of the Spirit, so that I might love and know the joy in Your presence, All-Holy God.

Thanks. I love You. Have mercy on us all and me, a sinner.

Love, Mike

May 25, 1995

Mike, know that I AM with you always.

Receive me, sick and sinful yet hopeful, worried about eating and sleeping. Help me to trust and to worship You in fear and to call on Your love and openness.

Thanks. I love You. Have mercy on me.

Love, Mike

May 29, 1995

Mike, I will ask My Father to give you another helper to be with you always, the Spirit of Truth.

I call upon you, for you will answer me, O God.

I shall be content in your presence.

Lord,

Receive me tonight, anxious, worried, thankful, and hopeful. Grant me the gift of the Holy Spirit, that I might be content resting in Your loving presence.

Thanks. I love You. Have mercy on me.

Love, Mike

May 30, 1995

Mike, call on Me in fear and love, and I'll save you. I will ask My Father to send you another Helper to be with you always—the Holy Spirit. Be content and joyful and thankful to be called into My love.

Lord, I am broken tonight—physically sick from anorexia, stomachache, and sore muscles and , butt; mentally, emotionally, and spiritually exhausted; feeling angry and discouraged and so mixed up!

Tonight, receive me, my sinful self. Thanks for calling me into Your love and offering me Your gift, O Holy God, how glorious is the hope to which You call me in You.

Thanks, Have mercy on me, a sinner. I love You.

Mike

May 31, 1995

Mike, praise and love Me. In that is the true life.

Lord, I love You. Lord, my strength, my deliverer. My being proclaims Your greatness, O Lord, my God, and my spirit rejoices in You, O God, my Savior.

Receive me tonight. Thanks, I am feeling much better. You are saving and helping me—thanks. I love You. I have a long way to go, but I am finding that You are with me deep inside and that You love me as I am. Deep within, You call me to love.

Have mercy on me, a sinner. Thanks. I love You.

Mike

June 1, 1995

Mike, I will set you free and rescue you because I love you.

I will ask My Father to send you another helper to be with you always, the Spirit of Truth.

Dear Lord,

Receive me tonight, as the first step. Lord, I am powerless and helpless and unable to deal with the consequences of my sinfulness and brokenness. My whole life is unmanageable and out of control. I am physically and spiritually sick, and I need You. I am broken—stomachache, bleeding, hunger, exhaustion, anger, sadness, and despair. I cannot reach the image I set for myself in weight loss, and I'm beating myself up over it. I don't even weigh 105, and yet I'm fat. I am sick and obsessed and sinful, and totally overwhelmed and scared. I can't make it on my own, and I need You. I want to come to know You. Grant me the grace to surrender and trust You, Your love and Your presence, moment by moment, are helping me to open up.

Lord, have mercy on me. Thanks. I love You

Love, Mike

I made you for myself. Your heart will be restless until you rest in me. I will rescue you, save you, and free you. Call on Me, for I AM with you.

June 2, 1995

They crucified Him.

Mike, I AM your God, lover, and savior.

Lord, receive me tonight, broken, exhausted, and angry. I can't seem to get what I want—weight loss. I'm so sad I feel like crying, I have had gas, cramps, and bloating pain all day, and I'm scared and helpless. I am too broken and sinful, and I can't make it.

Lord, save me. You are my only hope. I have no life, value, meaning, or existence without You. Thanks for being there for me and for being with me and listening to me babbling. I am sorry. Forgive me for giving up, and for being proud and selfish. Tonight I offer You my body, mind, and soul. You gave Yourself up to death so that I might live, yet I am a sinner.

Have mercy on me. Thanks. I love You.

Love, Mike

June 12, 1995

Jesus,

Thanks for helping me make it through the past three days. I was really hurting and discouraged. I did not feel I could deal with my life anymore.

Thanks for helping me realize how much I need You. I am a sick, weak, and sinful man, and I am not strong enough to handle my problems. In my weakness, I'm beginning to truly know my need for You. With You I can make it, for You are my God, and You love me, and You are more powerful than my sickness and problems.

Thanks for helping me change. Help me to continue to change. Help me to pray, love, and live simply, one day at a time, with You. Thank You.

I love You.

June 13, 1995

Jesus, thanks for helping me make it. Thanks for helping me change. I'm struggling, and change is not easy, but it is worth it. Help me continue to grow. Thanks. I love You.

June 14, 1995

Jesus, I thank You for a new beginning. I thank You for helping me change. Change is painful but worth it. I need You to be with me and help me to continue to grow. Help me to pray, love, and live simply, one day at a time, with You. Thanks. I love You.

June 18, 1995

Jesus, thanks for being with me. Thanks for helping me change. Thanks for healing me. Change is not easy, but it is worth it, and I am beginning to change. I need You, and without You my life would have no hope or meaning. Help me believe in You and Your love for me. Help me depend on You and trust You. Help me not worry or be upset. Help me seek You and Your Father's kingdom before all else. Help me realize that You are the way, truth and life. Thanks. I love You.

June 27, 1995

They crucified Him.

Father, forgive them, they do not know what they are doing.

Mike, call upon Me and I will answer you.

Dear Lord,

I call upon You, for You will answer me, O God.

I'm sick tonight, Lord, stomachache, gas, anxiety about anorexia, feelings of brokenness. I don't know if I'll be ok, I'm so messed up, physically, emotionally, and spiritually. I feel like I'm beyond hope.

Yet maybe this is the answer—my sickness, brokenness, and sinfulness are beyond help, but through my own powerless and poverty I can come to know my need for You.

Thanks. Have mercy on us and on me, a sinner. I love You.

Mike

June 28, 1995

Mike, call upon Me, and I will answer you. I AM your God. I will ask My Father, and He will give you another Paraclete to be with you, the Spirit of Truth.

Dialogue 2: 1995

June 3, 1995

They crucified Him.

Mike, I have rescued you and set you free because I love you. I died for you, and I want you to be Mine.

Dear Lord,

Receive me tonight on the feast of Pentecost. From the cross, You tell me that You will free and rescue Yourself. Lord, I too must accept dying and rising if I want to grow. I must die to my selfish and sinful ways daily and rise to Your love. Lord, grant me the grace to surpass whatever blocks me from the gift of Your spirit.

O Savior, Holy Spirit, Lord, have mercy on me, a sinner. Thanks. I love You.

Mike

June 4, 1995 Sunday Pentecost

Peace.

He showed them His hands and side.

Peace, as the Father has sent Me so I send you.

He breathed on them and said, "Receive the Holy Spirit."

I AM your God, savior, lord, lover, and best friend. I AM with you and in you and there for you always. Call on Me often in fear and in love.

O Lord,

You are my rock and redeemer. I offer You me tonight, broken and sinful, powerless to handle my own problems, worried, tired, angry, and discouraged. Lord, have mercy on me. In showing Your hands and Your side, You showed the way to peace and wholeness, to self-sacrificial love, to the death of sin and selfishness. Lord, I am weak and afraid; grant me the gift of the Holy Spirit so that I might love.

Thanks. Have mercy on me, a sinner. I love You.

Mike

June 5, 1995

I will ask My Father. He will give you another, the Holy Spirit, to be with you always. You can recognize Him because He remains within you.

Mike, find strength to love in calling on Me. I will save you and reveal Myself to you.

Dear Lord,

Praise be to You, Lord, for we are strong in the name of the lord our God, who answers us when we call him.

Receive me tonight, hopeful and hurting, knowing I am sick and sinful and wanting to change. I offer You me tonight, worried about changing and about dying to myself. Grant me grace in the Holy Spirit, that I might love.

Have mercy on me. Thanks. I love You.

Mike

June 6, 1995

Mike, have courage. Choose to respond to love, to be open and not caught up in the world. I will ask My Father to send you a helper, the Holy Spirit, to be with you and in you. Call on Me in humility, praise, and love, and I will save you.

Praise be to You, O Holy One. Thanks for the gift of Your life, Yourself, and Your Holy Spirit. Praise be to You, O Holy God, for being with and in me. Slowly I'm growing in Your love, aware of my sinfulness, brokenness, and need for redemption. Thanks for telling me to need You and for giving Yourself to me. Receive me tonight, worried, afraid, and hoping to grow in Your love.

Thanks. I love You. Have mercy on me, a sinner.

Mike

June 7, 1995

Mike, if you love Me, you will keep the commandments I've given you and be true to My word. Love Me, Mike. In loving, you will come to know Me.

Lord, have mercy on me, a sinner.

You called me to holy, sacred, loving relationship with You, O Most Holy God, and I rejected it and refused to love. I put my vanity before You, sinner and broken person that I am. I sought to get what I wanted through prayer—weight loss, image, health—as if I were giving a wish list to Santa. O Lord, forgive me for abusing the holy friendship You offer me. I am sinful, broken, powerless, and incapable of true love. Thank You, Lord for pointing this out to me. Forgive me, continue in Your love, and have mercy on me. I thank and praise You because You love me as I am, a selfish, sick, and sinful creature.

Lord have mercy on me, a sinner. Thanks. I love You.

Mike

June 7, 1995

Anyone who loves Me will true to My Word.

My God, My God, why have you abandoned Me?

Mike, get to know Me by letting Me tell you about My love for you. Listen to My Word. I took on and defeated sin and death, and I know the abandonment you feel. I love you so much that I chose to suffer in person and die for you. Let Me love you now, this moment.

Lord,

Receive me tonight, exhausted, sick, and thankful for Your revealing Yourself to me.

Thanks. Have mercy on me. I love You.

Mike

June 8, 1995

The Holy Spirit whom the Father sends in My name will instruct you on everything and remind you of all that I have told you.

Mike, take the time to get to know Me, your God, savior, and lover. The Holy Spirit will guide and empower you to love.

Dear Lord,

Tonight I feel closeness to You, joy and relief. For two days, I've really struggled with my past—sexuality, money, starvation. I've closed myself off and not always been there for Alice and others. I had knots in my stomach, I felt dirty and bad, but I called on You for mercy and You answered, Your forgiveness and healing were overpowering. Praise be to You for Your loving, gentle shepherd, for Your caring for me, a stupid, mixed-up, unfaithful and sinful lamb. Praise be to You for calming my fear and guilt and being with me. Thanks for opening me to You, Your Father's love, and the awesome gift of the Holy Spirit.

Continue to have mercy on me, a sinner. Thanks. I love You.

Mike

June 9, 1995

They crucified Him.

Father, forgive them.

Michael, Michael, My broken, sick, sinful, and loveable child. I forgive you, for I AM your God, crucified savior, best friend, and lover. I want you to know Me, and My mercy and My love. I died for love of you, and I want you to be Mine. Believe, slow down, and experience Me.

Out of my depths, I've called and cried to You, O My God, and You, O Lord, have heard and answered me. Truly with You all is pardon and forgiveness.

I'm exhausted and broken and guilty, and I feel like garbage tonight. Sinful and sad, I called to You, and You answered. Perhaps I don't listen enough, and too often get stuck in my own misery. Forgive me, receive me, and grant me the grace to acknowledge my sinfulness and my need for You, because my life is unmanageable. Grant me the grace to die to my selfishness and be open to knowing You better, O Holy One, my Crucified Lord. Thanks for the gift of Your love.

Have mercy on me, a sinner. I love You.

Mike

June 10, 1995

They crucified Him.

Father, forgive them.

Michael, I forgive you and love you. I AM with and in you. Believe, and come to know Me and My love.

Praise be to You, Most Holy Lord, My Crucified Lover and Savior. Even though I walk in the valley of darkness, I shall not fear, for You are with me, Most Blessed and Holy One. Receive my thanks and praise and total self tonight, Lord. Thanks. You are my God, lover, and savior. I'm beginning to open up and experience Your forgiveness and mercy and love.

Thanks. Continue to have mercy on me, a sinner. I love You.

Mike

June 11, 1995

I will ask My Father to give you another helper, the Spirit of Truth, to be with you always. You can recognize Him because He will remain with you and within you.

Mike, call on Me in humble, loving, trusting, fear and awe. I will continue to reveal Myself to you. Be open and believe.

Lord,

Receive me tonight, thankful and slowly opening up to You. It is awesome. Help me continue to open up to You, O Most Holy One, and experience Your mercy. Receive me in my exhaustion, and sickness, in my worries over my stomach, weight, and butt. Thanks for helping me become a more loving person, forgive me for still being selfish, and grant me the grace to continue to experience Your love.

Have mercy on me, a sinner. Thanks. I love You.

Mike

June 12, 1995

Mike, anyone who loves Me will be true to My word. My Father will love him, and We will come to Him and make a dwelling place for him.

Lord, My God,

You are my loving shepherd, and I am broken, sinful lamb. I'm called to love You, Lord, yet I don't know how to love. In the past, my love has been driven by fear and guilt. Lord, teach me to love, perhaps as You do for.

God wants us to be revealed to Himself, for God made man, who didn't know sin to be sin, so that in Him he might bare the very holiness of God.

Lord, You did it for my sins because You love me. You offered me a chance to take part in Your love. That is the only way I can love—in willingness to be built up by You, Lord. Praise be to You and Your love. Receive me tonight.

Thanks. Have mercy on me. I love You.

Mike

June 13, 1995

Michael, I AM your loving savior. Be reconciled to Me and My Father through the power of the Holy Spirit. I want you to be mine.

I AM your loving friend. I AM always with you, and you need fear nothing, for I am with you and at your side. For your sake I, who didn't know sin, became sin to defeat it and so that in Me you could share in the very holiness of God.

Lord, I am thankful tonight. I've really struggled with weight and anorexia. Grant me the grace to love with my illness and open to You and Your limitless, personal, passionate love for me. Receive my broken, sinful, self tonight, and continue to have mercy on me.

Thanks. I love You.

Mike

June 14, 1995

Mike, let Me be your loving Shepherd and give you all the love you need and more. You shall want for nothing. Let Me guide you through the gifts of the Holy Spirit Whom the Father sent in My name. We will make Our dwelling place in you. I love you and want you for Myself. I, Who did not know sin, became sin so that you might share in My glory—life eternal with the living God.

Praise be to You, O Holy Crucified Lord. Receive me tonight, a sinner and sick man with problems and worries. I offer You praise. Thanks for being my savior and revealing Yourself to me. Continue to have mercy on me, a sinner. I love You.

June 15, 1995

Peace, Mike, I AM your loving God. Let me shepherd, guide, and love you, that you may find peace in Me. You shall want nothing and have nothing to fear. I love you and want you to let Me reveal Myself to you. I who didn't know sin became sin that in and with Me you might experience the glory of life and God.

Dear Lord,

All praise and thanks to You. Receive me tonight, tired, stressed out, and worried about my health, my weight, my butt and insomnia problems. Thanks for helping me be open to Your healing peace and love.

It's ok to be me. I'm not bad. Sick and sinful yes, but also good—created by You with love. You loved me so much that You set me free to know You and Your love and peace. Help me to see that Your peace is not the absolution of trials but the experience of Your love deep within me.

Thanks. I love You. Continue to have mercy on me, a sinner.

Love, Mike

June 16, 1995

They crucified Him.

Father, forgive them.

Mike, be reconciled to Me.

God made Him who didn't know sin, to be sin so that in Him we might become the very holiness of God.

Mike, I love you and desire to have you know Me and share in the holiness and the life of My Father, Me, and the Holy Spirit. I died for the love of you. Accept Me as your God, savior, and lover.

Lord,

Accept me tonight, a sick, stressed, and tired sinner. I thank You for the awesome call to reconciliation with You, Most Holy One. All praise be to You, Most glorious God, Savior and Lover. I offer You me. Thanks for healing me and opening me up to You. Grant me the gift to be open to You and the life You offer.

Thanks. I love You, Lord. Continue to have mercy on me, a sinner.

Love, Mike

June 17, 1995

They crucified Him.

Father, forgive them.

Be reconciled to me, Michael. I want you to be mine. I love you and want you to know Me and My love for you. Be My lover, and believe that I love you infinitely. I died for you.

Wow.

Lord, praise be to You, O Holy Son of God, My Love, My Savior, My Life and God. Thanks for opening me to You. Receive me tonight, exhausted and worried yet thankful. You empower me with Your love.

On the eve of the feast of Your most precious body and blood, I pray for forgiveness for being closed. I pray for help to be more open to experiencing You.

Thanks. Continue to have mercy on me, a sinner. I love You.

Mike

June 18, 1995, Feast of Corpus Christi

Take this and eat it—this is My body, which will be given up for you.

Dear Lord,

Help me to listen and to open up. I need and want Your help. Daily You give Yourself to me, desiring me to let You in and let You love me.

Lord, forgive me. I am so preoccupied with so much junk that I'm often closed to You, Lord, until I slow down and think and begin to listen. I am in awe. You, Most Holy God, became one of us to die for us. You sacrificed Yourself for me, giving Yourself up, body and blood, on the cross and in the Eucharist. You offer me, an unworthy sinner, the gift of Your body and blood, no mere symbols but the Word made flesh. Lord, let me open up and let You in so that You may dwell within me. Receive me, broken and worried, and heal me.

Have mercy on me, a sinner. Thanks. I love You.

Love, Mike

June 18, 1995, Feast of Corpus Christi, evening

Take this and eat it—this is My body. This is My blood, the blood of the covenant to be poured out on behalf of many for the forgiveness of sins.

Michael, I know you are a sinner. That's why I became human: to reconcile you to My Father. I love you, and on your own you cannot make it. You were a broken sinner, but with and in Me— through My body and blood—you can be forgiven, healed, and loved. It's ok—I AM with you and I forgive you. Continue to repent and open up to Me.

Lord, all praise to You Who didn't know sin and became sin, Who giving Your Body and shed Your Blood so that many, including me, might be forgiven and share in Your life.

O Most Holy One, I denied my brother on the street today. I was too busy, too tired, too personal, too selfish. I am so wicked and sinful—I need a savior. I need You, not only in my anorexic, anxious, emotional problems, but as a broken, selfish sinner. I need Your forgiveness, my Lord. Help me to believe You love me, and grant me the grace to truly pray, Lord, Christ, Savior.

June 19, 1995

Mike, slow down and listen. I AM revealing Myself to you. In the quiet, in My word, and through the sacrifice that reconciled you and brought the forgiveness you seek, open up to receive My body and blood. I AM your loving savior.

Thanks, and praise You, Lord, I'm slowing down, a little, and I'm open to You revealing Yourself to me. Receive me and my worries tonight. I'm running out of juice, I'm anxious about weight and sleep. Grant me the growing trust I need to slow down and open myself to experiencing You, O Most Holy One.

Thanks. I love You. Continue to have mercy on me, a sinner.

Love Mike

June 20, 1995

Mike, take this and eat it. This is really My body. Mike, continue to slow down and listen. Receive Me. I want you to know Me, for with Me you shall want nothing. I am your God and your all.

Lord,

Receive me tonight, tired, stressed, and worried, about food, money, weight, guilt, and about my brother. Have mercy on him. He's hurting and he needs You, just like me.

Thanks for revealing Yourself to me. Help me slow down further and open all my prayers to You, O God. You died for me and us. Forgive me for lacking humility, awe, and reverence for the great and holy gift You made of Yourself to be my savior.

Thanks for loving me so much. I love You. Have mercy on me, a sinner.

Love Mike

June 21. 1995

Take this and eat it, this is My body.

Mike, I give you Me because I love you and want you to know Me and My mercy. Slow down and listen. I'll refresh, renew, empower, and heal you. I will love you and you will want for nothing.

Lord, receive me tonight, broken down, exhausted by my problems, plagued by worries and fears about eating, weight, health, butt, life, family. Forgive me for not being open in awe and appreciation of the gift of You give me daily. Help me open up to You.

Thanks. I love You. Have mercy on me, a sinner.

Love, Mike

June 22,1995

Mike, take this and eat it. This is My body. Receive Me and be open, slow down, and listen—with Me you shall want for nothing.

Lord, receive me—worried and struggling with eating, health, and sleep. Thanks for revealing Yourself to me, wow, it is awesome. O Most Blessed, Glorious, Savior, God, You freed me Yourself, You satisfied my hunger, praise be to You. Forgive me for failing so many times to show reverence to You. Continue to nourish, heal, and love me.

Thanks. Have mercy on me, a sinner.

Love, Mike

June 23, 1995

They crucified Him.

Father, forgive them.

Mike, I died that you might be forgiven and freed, and so that I could share Myself with you and reveal Myself to you. Slow down, listen, and let Me love you.

Praise and glory to You, O Most Holy Crucified God. Praise be to You who reveal the love of God to me, a sick, broken, sinful man. Continue to have mercy and reveal You to me.

I offer You me tonight, a sick and stressed sinner. I love You and want to know You. Live and love through me, O Most Holy One.

Thanks. Have mercy on me, a sinner. I love You.

Mike

June 24, 1995

They crucified Him.

Father, forgive them.

Mike, I died for you. I AM your God, lover, and crucified savior. I Who don't know sin became sin to defeat it, and to gain forgiveness for you, that you might come to know Me and receive Me. I forgive you. Continue to call on me in your brokenness.

Dear Lord,

Have mercy on me, a guilty sinner.

This is who I am tonight. Forgive me for my anger at Alice. In my sickness, I am not open. I am trying to take better care of myself—to see others, to reach out, and she is sick and fading and not herself. I feel like it is my own fault—I see her losing weight and I resent it, and I feel she likes having that over my head. I am not what I used to be, not there for her all the time. She claims to understand that I have my own life to live, yet I feel guilty. I feel that if I weren't so messed up through my own errors, I could be there for her and others. And even for myself.

Lord, forgive me. I am doing the best I can. But I feel guilty leaving my mom to see Alice. Save me from resenting Alice, who like me is a broken child of Yours. I love her and I am upset with myself, not her, because I am the one who messed up. She is a loving person and has isolated herself from many people, and I have done the same. She is a gruff old child of Yours. Help me to love her the best I can. I know I can grow in love through her.

Receive me tonight. Have mercy on us and on me, a sinner, Thanks. I love You.

Mike

June 25, 1995

Take this and drink it. This is the cup of My blood, to be poured out on behalf of you, so that your sins can be forgiven. Do this in memory of Me.

Mike, I who did not know sin became sin, sacrificing Myself on the cross for you. I will redeem you from sin and inequity. I am the vine, and you are the branch—live on in Me as I do in you. I am your life.

I want to heal you, forgive you, love you, and live through you. Open up to me.

Dear Lord,

I am hurting tonight, I want to experience Your forgiveness, but I feel like crying. I've been tormented by anxiety, fear, anger, self-hatred, disappointment, and helplessness. I am so hard on myself, Lord, dirty, disgusting, selfish, sick, unforgiving, and beyond help.

I am ashamed that I have no control, and I take it out with my weight. I am so sick, with no desire to getting better for fear of being like I used to be. Forgive me Lord, Crucified and Risen

God.

Have mercy on me, a sinner. Thanks. I love You.

Mike

June 26, 1995

Mike, take this and drink it. This is the cup of My blood, to be shed for you so that your sins might be forgiven. Do this in memory of Me. Live on in Me as I do in you. By living in Me, who didn't know sin but became sin to sacrifice myself for your sins, you share in the forgiveness I have given all people.

I praise You, O Most Holy Glorious Savior. By dying and rising and living in me, You offer me forgiveness and reconciliation and a new life. Thanks. I love You. Receive me tonight, exhausted, thankful, and in love with You.

Thanks. I love You. Have mercy on me, a sinner.

Love, Mike

June 27, 1995

Mike, Live on in Me as I do in you. I shed My blood to gain you forgiveness. All you must do is ask. Tell me you are sorry, and I will forgive you. Open up to me.

Lift up, o gates, your lintels. Reach up, you ancient poet, that the King of Glory might come in.

Lord, I am sorry for being selfish and rejecting Your loving forgiveness. Thanks for dying and forgiving me and giving Yourself to me. Grant me the grace to open my mind and love You. Receive me tonight, Lord, King of Glory, all praise be to You.

I love You. Thanks. Continue to have mercy on me, a sinner.

Love, Mike

June 28, 1995

Mike, live on in Me. I chose you, I forgive you, and I love you. I want to live in and through you—let Me.

Lord, Lover, God my Savior.

You pardon all my guilt, great as it is, for Your name's sake. All praise be to You for forgiving me and living in me with love. Thanks.

Today, I am experiencing You as my savior. I am forgiven because of Your sacrifice, perfect and holy and offered to me. You live in me, You forgive me, You cleanse me and guide me to use the gifts You have given me. May I use what You have given me in Your glory.

I love You. Thanks. Have mercy on me

Love, Mike

P.S. Thanks for the gift of my health. My doctor's report was great.

June 29, 1995

Mike, live on in Me as I do in you. Its ok. I AM your loving savior and God. With Me you shall want for nothing.

Lord,

Receive me tonight, exhausted and thankful. I am slowly opening up to You and to the power of Your love Thanks for loving me, forgiving me, and dying to save me. Thanks for filling me with Your life every day. Thanks for giving me the grace to "love through" my guilt over Alice. Receive me tonight.

Thanks. I love You. Have mercy on me, a sinner.

Love, Mike

June 30, 1995

Father, forgive them, they do not know what they are doing.

Mike, I forgive you. I love you. I AM your savior.

Lord,

I acknowledge my sin to You. I confess my faults to You, O Lord, and You take away the guilt of my sins. Thanks, Lord, my Crucified God, Lover, and Savior. Receive me tonight and continue to reveal Your mercy and love through me.

Thanks. Have mercy on me, a sinner. I love You.

Mike

July 1, 1995

They crucified Him.

Father, forgive them.

Mike, I forgive you.

Lord, with You is forgiveness that You might be revealed. Receive me tonight, broken, exhausted, and anxious, a sinner in love with You, my Crucified Lover, Savior, and God.

Continue to have mercy on me, a sinner. Thanks. I love You.

Mike

July 2, 1995

As My Father loved Me, so do I love You. Live on in my love.

Be humble and fear before Me. I will pardon your guilt, as great as it is.

Praise be to You, my Crucified, Risen Lover, my God and Savior. Receive me tonight, a broken and grateful sinner in need of Your mercy and wanting to know You better. Thanks for forgiving and loving me. I love You.

Continue to have mercy on me, a sinner. Thanks.

Love, Mike

July 3, 1995

Mike, as My Father loves Me, so do I love you. Live on in my love through the gift of My Spirit. You are precious to Me, My broken, sinful, little friend.

Praise to You, O Most Holy One.

You forgave me, You love me, and You want me to be Yours in intimacy and let Your love pour out upon me and others. Wow. Praise to You. Thanks for this awesome vocation. I am in awe, humbled by the Your gift. Receive me tonight, sorry for my sins, anxious and worried, yet in love with You

Continue to have mercy on me, a sinner. Thanks. I love You.

Mike

July 4, 1995

Mike, as My Father has loved Me, I love you. Live on in My love through the gift of the Holy Spirit. Let Him guide you.

Praise be to You, O Most Holy Crucified and Risen Christ, my Lord, God, Best Friend, Lover, and Redeemer,

You are freeing me from the bondage of my sins and sickness. You are having mercy on me and revealing Your love to me. Lord, continue to reveal Yourself to me and through me. I need to share Your love with others—especially, today with my brother. Lord, guide me through the Holy Spirit.

Thanks. I love You. Have mercy on me, a sinner

Love, Mike

July 5, 1995

Mike, I will pardon your guilt, as great as it is. I forgive you for your sins. I, Who didn't know sin, became sin because I love you, My friend, and I died to offer you salvation—to offer you My life with the Father through the love of the Holy Spirit—to offer you My forgiveness, My love and the pure gift of Myself, because I love you. Accept Me. Accept My forgiveness and love as gifts, for you cannot earn them. Simply call on Me in fear and have healthy sorrow for your sins, and I will cleanse, forgive, love, and heal you, and I will reveal Me to you. I love you and want you to be Mine.

Dear Lord,

Forgive me tonight for failing to appreciate the awesomeness of Your sacrifice and Your love of me. Perhaps it is what I've heard of men dying for others, but in my sin I can't see perfectly unselfish acts. O Blessed Savior, purely and without reservation You subjected Yourself to annihilation for love of me. Thanks. Grant me the grace to be open to You and Your love. Receive me tonight, and have mercy on my brother and me. We really need You.

Have mercy on me, a sinner. Thanks. I love You.

Love, Mike

July 6, 1995

Mike, there is no greater love than this: that I laid down My life for you, My beloved friend, and give Myself to you daily. Take and eat this, it is My Body—My love for you knows no limits.

Dear Lord,

Receive me tonight, exhausted and anxious. Grant me rest and open my eyes, ears, mind, heart, and soul to Your infinite love for me and all people. Let me begin to love in, with, and through You, o my loving God. Thanks for having mercy on my brother.

Have mercy on all and on me, a sinner. Thanks. I love You.

Mike.

July 7, 1995

They crucified Him.

There is no greater love than mine for you. I died for you, hoping you would say yes to Me and My love for you.

Lord, Jesus, Christ, Son of God, have mercy on us and on me, a sinner.

Thanks. I love You.

Mike

July 8, 1995

They crucified Him. Father, forgive them.

Mike, I forgive you. Allow Me to love you.

Thanks, Lord, for forgiving me. You did it for me.

Thanks for helping me and my brother. You are so good, O Most Holy Crucified Lord. Praise be to You. Help me appreciate what You do for my brothers and sisters.

Continue to have mercy on us and on me, a sinner. Thanks. I love You.

Mike

July 9, 1995

Mike as My Father loved Me, so I love you. Let me love you. I loved you so much that I died for you. You didn't choose me, I chose you, that you may love as I love through the gift of My spirit.

Lord, redeem me and have pity on me, a sinner in need of You, and I will bless You and praise You in the assembly.

Lord, receive me tonight, exhausted. By my own power I am helpless and sinful. Grant me the gift of Your spirit. Grant me personal love and a relationship with You, so that I might share You and Your love with others.

Thanks. Have mercy on me, a sinner. I love You.

Mike

July 10, 1995

Mike, I AM your light and salvation. I AM your God and savior and lover. Do not fear anything, for I am with you and in you.

Thanks, Lord.

Receive me, in anxiety and fear. Help me to trust in You more. Continue to have mercy on me, a sinner.

I love You.

Mike

July 11, 1995

Mike, as My Father loves Me, so do I love you. Live on in love with Me. Fear Me, call on Me in awe and love, and I will save you.

Dear Lord,

Teach me how to live in love with You, O Holy God. Receive me tonight, broken and worn out, not making it on my own. Thanks for loving through me today. I'm exhausted and worn out, I'm so enslaved by my anorexia. I was up last night, drank too much juice, had the runs, and bleeding. I'm full of discouragement and exhaustion now, mental torment. Should I eat or not? This low-energy, slow-power routine of prayer, work, walk, church is unbearable. My home life is routine and regimented by anorexic survival demands. My day is filled with its consequences —exhaustion, stress, distractions from prayer; pain, gas, legs, head, stomach, butt. I feel guilt, shame, disengagement, anger, disappointment, hurt, and sadness. I'm so sick, so twisted and sinful.

Yet that is my strength if I can surrender to You, can give up control. I can't live and love without You. You give meaning to me, and without You I am empty, chasing unattended feelings. Help me, Lord, to surrender and admit my sin, to seek Your forgiveness and turn my life over to Your will. You have already defeated my foes and offered me salvation, life, love, healing, and victory. Save, me Lord. I need You.

Have mercy on me, a sinner. Thanks. I love You.

Mike

July 12, 1995

Mike, as My Father loves Me, so do I love you. Live on in love with Me. Don't be afraid. I love you, and I AM with you to help and protect you.

Lord,

Thanks for being there for me. I'm struggling with the ugly, sinful, sick, tormented part of myself. Continue to help me. Receive me tonight, broken, thankful, and growing more dependent on You and more in love with You.

Have mercy on me, a sinner. Thanks. I love You.

Mike

July 13, 1995

Mike, as My Father loves me, so do I love you—as you are. Live in love with Me. I will take care of you. I died for you. I AM in love with you.

Lord,

Receive me tonight, sick, exhausted, and anxious, yet thankful, hopeful, and relieved. I'm getting better by being more open to Your love and mercy.

It's been a rough day. I'm stressed out big time.

Thanks. I love You. Have mercy on me, a sinner.

Love, Mike

July 14, 1995

They crucified Him. Father, forgive them.

Mike, I will redeem you from all your iniquities. Open up to experience Me and My mercy and love for you.

Praise be to You, Crucified Lord, God and Savior.

Thanks for dying for me, forgiving me, and giving me Your love. Help me to open up to You. Receive me tonight, sick and anxious, with a sore throat.

Continue to have mercy on me, a sinner. Thanks. I love You.

Mike

July 15, 1995

They crucified Him.

Father, forgive them.

Mike, I have chosen you out of this world to be a witness to Me in the world.

Lord,

Receive me tonight, a broken sinner in need of You. Forgive me for being so caught up in my own problems and for my failure to be a witness to You. I am too scared to share, because I don't want to be labeled as a right-wing fanatic. But I feel the world's rejects. I am a coward, Lord, I know I am unworthy of Your call and too messed up to be a proper witness for You, the One True God, so I hide. But this is the time to stop hiding and take risks.

Lord, on my own I am too broken to be a witness to You. Grant me the gift of the Holy Spirit so that I might witness in love with You and my brothers.

Thanks for helping me pray and for having mercy on me, a sinner. I love You.

Mike

July 16, 1995

I have chosen you, Michael, out of this world to be a witness to Me.

Dear Lord,

Praise be to my Crucified Risen God, Redeemer, Friend, and Lover. Thanks for choosing me. Receive me tonight, sinful, anxious, and weak. On my own I am unable and unworthy to witness to You. But grant me the gift of Your spirit, Holy One, so that I might love.

Thanks. Have mercy on me, a sinner. I love You.

Mike

July 17, 1995

I have chosen you out of this world to be My witness. I have heard your pleading. I AM your strength in your weakness, and I will help and save you because I love you.

Lord,

Receive me tonight, exhausted, sick as a dog. I've had severe gas pains all day. I'm worn out and I know I can't make it on my own in life. It is good of You to choose me out of this world, because on my own, as St Augustine writes, I will self-destruct in misery. I know that I still resist Your will, Your way, and Your guidance, Lord. Receive me and my desire to be Yours through the Spirit's help to let go of the obstacles that close me off from You, my life.

Have mercy on me, a sinner. Thanks. I love You.

Mike

July 18, 1995

Mike, I know you are hurting, struggling, weak, and sinful. I will send Him, the Holy Spirit, to help you respond to my call.

Lord,

Receive me tonight, exhausted, anxious, wiped out, overwhelmed by my sinfulness and powerless and in need of You.

Have mercy on me, a sinner. Thanks. I love You.

Mike

July 19, 1995

Mike, I love you and want to share Myself with you. I will send the Holy Spirit to be with you and guide you to the truth—life in Me, the Living God.

Lord,

Receive me tonight, exhausted, hopeful, and longing for You.

Have mercy on me, a sinner. Thanks. I love You.

Mike

July 20, 1995

I will send the Holy Spirit to you.

Lord,

Accept me tonight. All glory to You, O Most Holy One. I'm broken, sinful, sick, and exhausted. I can't make it on my own. I need and want You to save me, Lord.

Have mercy on me, a sinner. Thanks. I love You.

Mike

Dedicate yourself to doing My will daily.

Lord,

You reveal Yourself to me. Help me listen, and grant me the grace to live and love Your will for me.

Mike

July 21, 1995

They crucified Him.

Father, forgive them.

Mike, be reconciled to God in Me, and accept My forgiveness. I call you to to pray constantly for union with Me and reconciliation for all. I call you to know Me and share Me in the world. Be a witness for Me and My love for all.

Lord,

Receive me tonight, broken, sick, tired, yet in awe at Your call and thankful for what You do for me. I am afraid, too, for I am weak and unworthy—grant me the grace to experience You and share You by loving and forgiving as You have done.

Have mercy on me, a sinner. Thanks. I love You.

Mike

July 22, 1995

Father, forgive them.

Mike, let Me forgive you. Let Me love you, and let Me love through you.

Lord,

Receive me tonight, exhausted, worried, and sinful, yet grateful. You are revealing Yourself to me, O Crucified Savior.

Have mercy on my brother, on us and on me, a sinner. Thanks. I love You.

Mike

July 23, 1995

Mike, call on Me. In Me you will find peace, and you will suffer. Trust in Me.

Lord,

Thanks for being my savior and lover. Receive me tonight, sinful and worried, and have mercy on me. Thanks. I love You.

Mike

July 24, 1995

Mike, My Father and I love you very much. You will suffer in this world—have courage and find peace in Me.

Lord,

Receive me tonight, exhausted, worried, sick, and afraid. Help me to trust and find courage in You. I'm worn out, Lord, and I can't make it. I am fearful and unworthy. My faith and trust are so weak. O Lord, help me to put my trust in You, now and whenever I call on You.

Thanks. I love You. Have mercy on me, a sinner.

Mike

July 25, 1995

Mike, I offer you eternal life. I offer you to know the One God, and to know Me, the Only Son, Jesus, sent to save you for life in and with Me.

Lord,

Receive me tonight, a sinner and weak, worried and tired. Help me attend to Your words and to Your presence with me now. And have mercy on us, my brother and me, a sinner. Thanks. I love You.

Mike

July 26, 1995

Mike, come to know Me even in your exhaustion, for I AM with you now. I offer you eternal life. I offer to let you know Me, Jesus, the only Son of God, your savior, lord and lover. I want you to be mine, and I AM here for you now.

Lord, receive me tonight. Help me to be open to You. I need and want You.

July 27, 1995

Mike, on your behalf I pray to My Father, as I pray for all that you all may be one in us, and that I may live in and through you.

Into Your hands, Lord, I entrust my spirit.

You will redeem me, O Faithful One. Grant me the grace to call on You in fear and in love. Lord, receive me tonight, tired and broken and unable to be one with my brothers and sisters in You. I need You and I want to experience the oneness in love that You offer. Praise be to You.

Have mercy on me. Thanks. I love You.

Mike

July 27, 1995

They crucified Him.

Father, forgive them.

Mike, I AM with you in your suffering. I died for you on the cross. I took on your brokenness, suffering, and sins, and defeated them. I offer you forgiveness and a personal love relationship with Me, your God.

Lord, into Your hands I surrender me tonight.

Help me, Lord. I want to give You me. But I'm afraid to let go. Continue to have mercy on me, a sinner.

Thanks. I love You.

Mike

July 28, 1995

They crucified Him.

Father, forgive them.

Mike, I died for you and your sins because I love you. Continue to confess your sins and to call on Me in your sinfulness. I will forgive you and reveal myself to you and through you. Rejoice in Me and My love.

Lord, receive me tonight, exhausted, worried, and anxious, but happy. I am in awe and I rejoice because You are revealing Yourself to me. Continue to forgive me.

Have mercy on me, a sinner. Thanks. I love You, Lord.

Mike

July 29, 1995

Mike, believe. Believe in Me and My loving care for you.

Lord, I am not worthy to receive You, but only say the word and I'll be healed.

Lord, grant me a strong faith. I am so weak in faith and trust, but with You I want for nothing.

Lord, receive me tonight, worried, anxious, and thankful. Praise be to You.

Have mercy on me, a sinner. Thanks. I love You.

Mike

July 31, 1995

Mike, I have chosen you to be mine. Wait for Me and rejoice in Me and trust Me. I love you!

Thanks, Lord. You saved me today. I had no chance for morning Mass, and You took care of it—St. John's at 11:00 A.M.

Receive me tonight. Thanks for giving me You and for forgiving me my failure to treasure the gift of You in my life.

Have mercy on me, a sinner. Thanks. I love You.

Mike

August 1, 1995

Blest is he who finds no stumbling block in Me. Accept me as your personal lord, savior, Lover, and God, now at this moment.

Lord, come into my heart.

I want You to be my God, savior, and lover. Receive me, exhausted and worried. I ate an egg today. I've been stressed and worried about whether You would get me through. Thanks.

I love You. Have mercy on me, a sinner.

Love, Mike

August 2, 1995

Blest is that man who finds no stumbling block in Me.

Lord, I am not worthy to receive You, but only say the word and I will be healed.

Dear Lord,

You came to save us. You are my savior—thanks. You save me daily in so many ways, physical, emotional, and spiritual, and it is awesome—thanks.

Listening to You this morning, I feel bad. You point out to me that I am like the Pharisees. Accepting You and Your understanding and love are a stumbling block for me. I resist You in my sins and sickness that I am unwilling to let go of. I am ashamed of my resistance, my pride, my vanity—I want what I want, my way, and I close You out.

Forgive me for rejecting You, my Crucified God, my lover, during prayer at Mass. I follow my sickness and I continue doing it my way, because I am terrified of changing. I need help, yet I reject it, and in rejecting it I reject You and Your call to know You and to be a witness to You. My choice to remain in my sickness injures my ability to respond to Your call. Forgive me Lord, for like the Pharisees I cling to what I want, to the way of life I am comfortable with. I am a sinner.

Have mercy on me. Grant me the grace to accept Your blessing and receive Your healing. Forgive me for being closed to Your call. I'm too caught up in the things about me to be open. Lord, forgive me, and help me. I need You and I want to know You more.

Thanks. Have mercy on me, a sinner.

Mike.

P.S. I love You.

August 2, 1995

Her many sins are forgiven because of her great love.

Your sins are forgiven. Go in peace.

Your faith is your salvation.

Lord, receive me tonight, exhausted and worried but thankful for Your help. Yes, in Your word You tell me how much You love me. Thanks. That is my hope and my life. I need You. Help me to spend time at Your feet, and to give You me as the penitent woman gave You herself.

Have mercy on me, a sinner. Thanks. I love You.

Mike

August 4, 1995

They crucified Him.

Father, forgive them.

Mike, I forgive you.

Lord, thanks for accepting me tonight, exhausted and humbled by Your love. Help me stand by You and be with You on the cross. Help me to see You in others, and have mercy on me. Thanks. I love You.

Mike

August 5, 1995

They crucified him.

Father, forgive them.

Mike, I AM your God. I became one of you and want to be one with you in love so much that I died for you!

Lord, thanks. I am in awe and humbled by You and Your love. Receive me tonight, anxious and hopeful. Continue to have mercy on me, a sinner. Thanks. I love You. Mike.

August 5, 1995

Her many sins were forgiven because of her great love.

Mike, let Me love you.

Lord, receive me. I'm so sinful, selfish, anxious, weak, and sick. I want to become a loving person. Lord, teach me to love with Your love. You have given me who I am. Grant me the grace to be a loving servant, giving what You have given me to others. Lord, help me

Thanks. I love You. Have mercy on me, a sinner.

Mike

P.S. Glory to You, Most Holy God.

Dear Lord,

Help me to become like the penitent woman, for I am a greater sinner than she. I must approach

You humbly and worship and love You and mourn my sinfulness, for Lord, I am so sinful. I put my anorexia before You, and I shut You and others out because I want to lose weight. I'm judgmental of others and ungrateful for all You do for me. I despise those who keep me from quiet time and Mass. If You had offered so much to anyone else, they would be a saint. I am messed up and don't want to change, Lord. I wonder even about closing the door to Your call and staying in my own head. It's a sick thought I want to lose, lose, lose. I'm not open to Your call and will for me, even though I've wanted so deeply for You to save me and still want it.

Lord, I'm sorry. I want to know You and serve You and lose, lose, lose, but I can't do it. I am trying. I offer You my struggle. Help me open up to Your grace. I can't handle my sinfulness, sickness, shame, guilt, and fear . You can—You did—on the cross You took on my sins and infirmities and defeated the evil that plagues me.

Lord, have mercy on me, a sinner. Thanks. I love You.

Mike

August 6, 1995

Mike, I forgive you, Your faith is your salvation. Peace. I love you and want you to be mine.

Thanks, Lord, for faith.

Accept the gift of me tonight, broken, worried, and sinful. Thanks for forgiving and being with me.

Have mercy on me, a sinner. Thanks. I love You.

Mike

August 7, 1995

Mike, your sins are forgiven. Your faith in Me is your salvation. I love you and want to be there for you, and I want you to be mine.

Lord,

I am broken tonight, and sad. Receive me as You did the woman who was known to be a sinner. I grieve and hurt for how sinful, selfish, twisted, and sick I am, and yet I rejoice because it is Your grace that gets me through the day. I need and want You, and I want to know You better. Forgive me for my failure to love, and help me be open to You.

Thanks. Have mercy on me, a sinner. I love You.

Mike

August 7, 1995

Follow Me.

Lord,

Help me to respond in faith and trust as Mary Magdalene did. You have done so much for me—healing, forgiving, loving, giving me life, yet I'm afraid to truly follow. I'm afraid to let go of what holds me back.

Lord, I offer my desire to follow You and accompany You. Receive me, a broken sinner and continue to have mercy on me.

Thanks. I love You.

Mike

August 8, 1995

With Me, you shall want for nothing. Follow Me as the woman I healed did.

They accompanied Me, assisted Me out of their means.

Lord,

Accept me tonight, exhausted, anxious, but grateful for Your healings. Help me to follow You and realize that You will take care of me. Help me to be a witness and a companion to You in this world.

Have mercy on me, a sinner. Thanks. I love You.

Mike

August 9, 1995

Mike, listen to Me. To you has been confided the mystery of the reign of God. You are blessed.

Dear Lord,

Accept me, exhausted and stressed, hurting my co-workers. Help me to listen and accept Your guidance. We need You. Thanks for confiding in me and loving me so much.

I love You. Have mercy on us and on me, a sinner.

Love, Mike

P.S. Forgive me for getting mad at the boss. Have mercy on us.

August 10, 1995

Mike, believe in Me. Trust My word. Persevere in loving, and I will save you. Trust Me with your life and problems, and I will guide you through this. I love you, Mike.

Dear Lord,

Receive me today. Thanks for revealing Yourself to me, Most Holy Lord. You showed me how much You love me, and yet my faith is weak. Lord, grant me the grace to persevere in Your love.

Forgive me for my selfishness and pride and for getting mad at my boss. She is a broken person like me, who needs You. She needs to be loved just as I do and just as my co-workers do. Last night, talking with Linda, I began to cry. All I want is to be loved, to be held. I hugged Valerie. The pain my boss is inflicting on my co-workers and friend is sick. They are all upset, and I am caught between them and unsure what to do. I don't have the answer to the problem, but You do.

Lord, so often I don't trust. Today I offer my desire to be guided by You. I believe You will give me the grace to persevere in loving them. Help us all, Lord. We are a needy and broken people, marred by sin, and You have the power to save us. Lord, help me to be open to Your guidance today, You the shepherd, me the little dumb sheep. May I call on Your name and be guided down the right path, knowing that You love me, that You free me from my sins by Your own blood.

I'm too sinful to love, but in You I am forgiven, loved and able to love. Thanks. Praise be to You, Most Holy Word of God.

Lord have mercy on us and me, a sinner. Thanks. I love You.

Mike

P.S. Lord, accept me tonight. Thanks for saving faith and trust. Thanks for helping me to trust You with my problem, for trusting You pays off!

Have mercy on me, a sinner. Thanks.

August 11, 1995

They crucified Him.

Father, forgive them.

Mike, I forgive you. Let Me into your heart to heal and love you. I want you.

Lord,

Thanks. Receive me tonight, anxious and hopeful. You are so good to me.

Have mercy on me, a sinner. Thanks. I love You.

Mike

August 12, 1995

They crucified Him.

Father, forgive them.

Mike, I accept your apology and your call for mercy. Please accept my forgiveness and mercy.

Praise to You, Holy God, for forgiving me.

Accept me tonight, worried, sick, sinful, and grateful. Thanks. I love You. Have mercy on me, a sinner.

Love, Mike

August 13, 1995

Mike, I love you, and I free you daily from your sin by My own blood.

Lord,

Thanks. Praise be to You, O Glorious God. You rescued me from my anxiety and shame today. Accept me tonight. I love You, Lord. Continue to have mercy on me, a sinner .Thanks for forgiving and helping me and for shedding Your blood for me.

I love You.

Mike

August 14, 1995

Mike, I call you to be My brother in love—a person who hears Me, the Word of God, and acts upon it. First, believe that I love you and send My blood to free you from your sins, so that you can be mine in love.

Thanks. Accept me tonight, anxious and tired, and guide me, Lord. Have mercy on me, a sinner. Thanks. I love You.

Mike

August 15, 1995

Mike, I AM here for you. Rejoice in your need for Me. Become My brother in love. I died to free you for Me.

Thanks, Lord, receive me tonight, exhausted and anxious, and have mercy on me, a sinner. Thanks. I love You.

Mike

August 15, 1995

My Mother and brothers are those who hear the word of God and act on it.

Mike, I call you out of bondage and the darkness of sin into the light of My love. I shed My blood to free you. Accept My forgiveness and My call to be My brother. I reveal Myself to you in My word—listen and be guided in love by Me.

Lord,

Accept me tonight. I'm sick and I need You. I'm in pain—the gas from anorexia hurts bad. I've lost weight, my stomach muscles are weak and can't pass. The pain makes me feel like a little old man, yet I am still determined to lose weight. I want to get along with medical people.

Lord, I am messed up and offer myself to You today. Thanks for forgiving me and for dying to set me free and for calling me to be Your brother. Lord, I'm unworthy. Help me listen to You and be guided by You, as Your mother Mary was.

Lord, have mercy on me, a sinner. Thanks. I love You.

Mike

August 16, 1995

Master, Master, we are lost.

Where is your faith?

Mike, believe in Me and My love for you. Believe in My power and desire to save you as I did with My disciples in the storm on the lake.

Lord,

My life is a storm. Help me to remember and know that You are with me. Accept me tonight, Lord, physically, emotionally, and spiritually broken. I'm sick and sinful and I need Your help to in You and Your power and desire to save me.

Thanks. Have mercy on me, a sinner. I love You.

Mike

Mike, it is ok. I AM with you.

Dear Lord,

Receive me in my anxiety and worries tonight. It was a rough day. My stomach is better, yet for the first time in weeks I passed blood going to bathroom. I'm scared and upset.

Help me to trust in You. I'm weak and tired from too many failures and disappointments. I'm tired and sick and I don't want to change. I'm sorry. I feel guilty because I should be unselfish in giving myself to You and others, yet I fight it with my anorexia. At church, the parish nurse introduced herself and said she was worried about me. She asked about my weight loss. I said I was ok. I was lying, but I felt like telling the truth—I'm sad and I don't want to die with it.

I'm tired of taking Alice's garbage out. It's too much right now. I didn't sleep well, and I fell down yesterday. I'm physically exhausted. And I'm emotionally stressed. A client made vague threats that if he was drinking he might hurt a co-worker. I didn't throw him out, and now I feel guilty. My judgment is off. I should be protecting my co-workers.

Lord, I offer You my failures tonight. Right now, I am a lot like Your disciples in the boat—lacking faith and trust. Grant me trust in You, O Holy God, my Lover and Savior. Be with me always. Have mercy on Bob, Julie, Linda, Tom, Sue, Jill, and Alice, and on my family, and Lord, have mercy on me, a sinner.

Thanks. I love You.

Mike

August 17, 1995

Master, we are lost.

Where is your faith?

Mike, have faith in Me. Trust Me. I AM with you and in you and want to save you for Myself to live in and with you.

Praise be to You, Holy Savior,

In many storms You have rescued me. Thanks.

Thanks for the gift of faith, of life. Thanks for Your giving and saving, time in and time out. You show me how much You are there for me.

Accept me tonight. I've had second thoughts about seeing Linda and Helen for help. Guide me and continue to help me at my work through my trust in You.

Thanks. Have mercy on me, a sinner. I love You.

Mike

August 18, 1995

They crucified Him.

Father, forgive them.

Mike, I forgive you. Be sorry for your sins and rejoice in My mercy and love. I died to save you.

Dear Lord,

"Happy is he whose faults are taken away."

Thanks for dying to set me free from my selfishness. Receive me tonight, sinful, broken, and anxious. And continue to have mercy on me, a sinner.

Thanks. I love You.

Mike

August 19, 1995

They crucified Him.

Father, forgive them.

Mike, I forgive you. I died to free you from your sins. Believe in My limitless love for you, My precious one.

Lord,

Accept me tonight, anxious and guilty. Forgive me for being selfish and untrusting. Have mercy on me, a sinner. Thanks.

Praise be to You Holy Savior. I confess my sins to You, and You forgive me and take away my guilt. Lord, help me learn from You and Your love. Help me grow from my sins and sickness. Help me to be humble before You and not believe that I know it all. Help me to forgive and love myself

Have mercy on me, a sinner. Thanks. I love You.

Mike

August 19, 1995

They crucified Him.

Father, forgive them.

I love you, Mike, and I want you for myself.

Dear Lord,

Thanks for Your gifts of forgiveness and love and mercy. Receive me tonight.

I feel peace, and perhaps it Your peace. I feel forgiven and hopeful and joyful, and it is You, Lord, not me—it is awesome. I can find the way despite all my problems, I'm very sick, I know, physically, emotionally, and spiritually, but I need You and I want You. I am a sinner, but in my brokenness You have revealed Yourself to me. Thanks.

Lord, guide me. I'm unsure what to do. I want to eat TX for my anorexia. I'm tired of my daily resistance to change. Perhaps I am imposing on You and neglecting Your call. But I am afraid to go further and I don't want to.

Yet how important is my choice? You died to give me freedom and love. I don't know what to do—I don't want to spend money or TX or time—and I'm stuck and don't want to wait for TX people. I can't return, because I'm afraid of my family's reaction. They want to see physical results, but I'm not willing to gain weight. Maybe it's better to withdraw and keep the door open to return. Right now I feel like I've had enough, though.

Lord, You gave Your life. I offer You my life today. I'm a broken man. Guide me and continue to have mercy on me, a sinner.

Thanks. I love You.

Mike

August 20, 1995

Mike, don't be afraid to love. Don't fear Me. I AM with you and in you, to save and love and heal you.

Lord,

Accept me tonight. Thanks for helping me get together with Bob. Forgive me for talking about Sue. Have mercy on both of them.

Accept me, anxious and worried—I have to talk to my boss Monday. Help me to trust in You. Help me to love.

Thanks. Have mercy on me, a sinner. I love You.

Mike

August 21, 1995

Daughter, your faith in Me has cured you—go in peace.

Mike, reach out and open up to Me so that I can heal you. Believe in Me and in My plan to save you. Believe how much I love you.

Lord,

Thanks. I got through the day. I "ratted" my boss out. Thanks for giving me the courage to move beyond my fears to do what is right and loving.

Now receive me, stressed and anorexic. I want to lose, to get down to 99. I got mad, someone said "hospitalization" and "no way I hit 99." I don't want to face my problems, forgive me. Thanks for making me need You and others. I'm so guilty and ashamed. Have mercy on me and on us all, and forgive me, Lord. Help me continue to grow in my need for You.

I love You. Have mercy on me, a sinner.

Love, Mike

August 23, 1995

Mike, fear is useless. What you need to do is to trust Me, for when I died on the cross for you I took on the sins and brokenness you've been plagued by your whole life. When you accept Me, you can make it, in My love.

Lord,

Accept me tonight, broken, exhausted, sinful, and imperfect. Come into my love. I want to receive You as my personal lord, savior, lover, and God. I can't make it without You. Without You, I am a failure. Forgive me for being so resistant in my anorexia.

Thanks. I love You. Have mercy on me, a sinner.

Love, Mike.

August 24, 1995

I AM with and in you, and I AM there for you. Trust Me, Michael, My beloved.

Praise be to You, Holy, Holy, Holy One. Accept me tonight, sick, impatient, sinful, and anxious, but thankful.

Thanks. Have mercy on me, a sinner. I love You.

Mike

August 25, 1995

They crucified Him.

Father, forgive them.

Mike, I forgive you. Trust in Me to save you.

My crucified God, Savior and Lover, my Lord. Thanks. You got me through a tough one. I'm doing great, I feel better, and I'm trusting more. Receive me tonight, anxious and nervous about my brother. Continue to heal me and have mercy on me. Thanks.

Love, Mike

August 27, 1995

They crucified Him.

Father, forgive them.

Mike, I your God love you, just as you are. I know that you are broken and sinful. You need Me in order to love. Let Me love you, and live in My love.

Lord,

Accept me tonight, worn out and anxious, resistant to my anorexia and feeling guilty about how miserably I fail to live a life of love. Thanks for loving me, Lord, it makes me happy inside to know Your love for me. I want to cry for joy. I feel like I am falling in love with You.

Thanks. Have mercy on me, a sinner. I love You.

Mike

Mike, love Me before all, but love others and love yourself. Learn to love yourself as I love you. Learn to see the beauty within you. Yes, you are a sinner, but you are also an icon—you were made in the image of God. You honor My Father by loving Me.

Praise be to You, O Lord, God.

Thanks. Accept me tonight, sinful, anxious, and wanting to love.

Have mercy on me, a sinner. Thanks. I love You.

Mike

Dialogue 3: 1995

August 28, 1995

They crucified Him.

Father, forgive them.

Mike, I am with you. I died for you. I forgive you and love you very much. Let me save you, moment by moment, to live in love with Me

Dear Lord,

Receive me tonight. Thanks for getting me up for Mass. I had no bleeding today, and a good sleep. I'm still a little tired and anxious.

I'm seeing Fr. T today—I don't know when I'm going, and I'm scared, Lord. I'm sick, sinful, anorexic, selfish, and resistant to therapy. I don't want to change—is this a sin? I want to call therapy, give money away, and have more time. I've lost weight, but 99 is my goal. Helen spoke of the hospital. Save me, Lord, but I don't want to gain or just maintain weight, only to lose it. It's so complicated. Right now I'm reducing my juice and food for "control." But I feel guilty. Am I running out on You? Am I killing myself?

Lord, have mercy on me. The past two weeks have been filled with anxiety and guilt, I've felt crazy, yet You've shown me Your powerful and saving love. It's gotten me through crisis after crisis.

Lord, I'm so fragile and broken. I feel bitter, but I know how weak I am in my sinfulness and brokenness. I am coming more and more to realize just how much I need You. Thanks, Lord. At the bottom of it all, I just want to be loved and have peace, and only in You and in love with You can I find this. Help me to open up and let Your love in. Forgive me, help me, and save me, Holy Crucified Savior. Open me to Your guidance, and grant me the grace to love. Forgive me for being proud, selfish, and resistant, and help me to be open to knowing You.

Thanks. Have mercy on me, a sinner. I love You.

Mike

August 29, 1995

Mike, let me love you. Love Me. Love others and yourself, and pray. I did not My will but yours, Father.

Lord,

Thanks. You answered me today. I am anxious and longing to know Your will. I seek guidance. You helped me listen and trust in You, and You answered me. Wow.

Lord, I'm growing in my love for You and in Your love for me. Thanks. Accept me tonight, broken, worried, anxious, and sinful, but in love with You.

Have mercy on me, a sinner. Thanks. I love You.

Mike

August 30, 1995

Father, not My will but Your will be done.

Mike, I forgive you for your sinning, lying, and failing to love yourself. Look to become more like Me, moment by moment, surrendering to Our Father in love. Trust Him. He and I love you greatly.

Lord,

Forgive me for lying, for covering up my anorexia and cheating at work—for signing up on time when I am five or ten minutes late. It's wrong, I've sinned, and I need to change and face the anorexia that has led me to a life of lying.

Lord, receive me tonight, broken and longing to be in need of You. Grant me the grace to depend on You. Thanks for teaching me and revealing Yourself to me. Have mercy on me, a sinner. Thanks. I love You.

Mike

August 31, 1995

Not my will but Your will be done, Father.

Mike, I want to save you and redeem you and free you from your guilt and sin and love you. Let Me.

Thanks, Lord for saving and healing and forgiving me. I called out in my sin and brokenness, and You answered me in love. Help me to listen in love to You, O Most Holy One, and forgive me for resisting Your will and choosing to stay anorexic, in my fear, pride, vanity, insecurity, and need to be in control. Help me become daily more like You and be open to Your Father's call to love. Continue to reveal Yourself to me and help me grow in love Accept me tonight.

I love You. Have mercy on me, a sinner. Thanks.

Love, Mike

September 1, 1995

They crucified Him.

Father, forgive them.

Mike, I forgive you. I love you and I want you to be mine.

Praise be to You, Crucified Lover, God and Savior.

Forgive me for being selfish and closed to You and others. Receive me tonight, worried and tired. Help me to be open to You. Help me become more like You.

Thanks. I love You. Have mercy on me, a sinner

Love, Mike

September 2, 1995

Not my will, but your will be done.

They crucified Him.

Father, forgive them.

Mike, follow after Me, trusting My Father's loving plan and seeking Me, that you might come to know and live in His will. I am with you and will help you. Let Me love you.

Praise be to You, O Crucified God, Savior and Lover.

Thanks for revealing Yourself to me in love, in Your heart. Accept me tonight, tired and anxious yet hopeful, and help me follow You and become a little more like You every day.

Thanks. I love You. Have mercy on me, a sinner.

Love, Mike

P.S. Lord, help me to be obedient by revealing Yourself to me in the Word. How blessed I am for all You do for me, and how unworthy I am. (A TV preacher said, "Live in My Word, trusting and obeying Me in love.")

September 3, 1995

Mike, he who humbles himself before Me, I will exalt in My love. Love Me first of all. Love others and yourself as I love you.

Praise be to You, Risen, Crucified, and Holy Savior.

You saved me today and gave me a small retreat in spirit by myself. Thanks for helping me. I am humbled by the awesomeness of Your love for me.

Thanks. I love You. Have mercy on me, a sinner.

Love, Mike

September 4, 1995

Let Me love you, and know My love. Experience My love for you. Love Me first of all. Love others and yourself.

Praise to You, O Holy Glorified One, My God, My Lover

Thanks. Accept me tonight, anxious and worried, but eager especially to grow in love with You.

Have mercy on me, a sinner. Thanks. I love You.

Love, Mike

September 5, 1995

Mike, love Me, others, and yourself. I know that you struggle. Be open to Me and My love for you. Experience Me.

Dear Lord,

Accept me tonight. I don't want to deal with my sexuality, the guilt and shame are too upsetting. I've spent most of my life anxious, thinking again and again, "I'm bad, I've done bad, I deserve punishment, I await it." I've lived in fear and worry, having to be perfect to make up for my sinfulness and ugliness and disgracefulness.

O Lord, forgive me for not loving myself as I am. Help me, Lord. I need You. I'm falling in love with You and Your love, with Your healing and teaching and loving me into health.

Continue to have mercy on me, a sinner. Thanks. I love You.

Mike

September 5, 1995 (PM)

Dear Lord,

I'm struggling. Guilt, anxiety, shame, anger, sickness—it doesn't take much to get my goat.

Bob is mad because I don't have an answering machine. I'm sad about writing to Jimmy—does he think I'm gay? I'm all upset about Alice. I tried to get the garbage out this week, but I've been working overtime, I'm tired and she won't let go. Yet she refuses to ask others for help—"It's me or nobody," and I'm guilty. I'll end up dropping it, I know. Accept my anger.

My tiredness is related to my anorexia. It causes my failure to love myself and my failure take care of my tired body. I keep giving in to guilt.

Lord, help me to handle my feelings and set health limits. Help me be good to myself and do what I can for others. I felt bad, and now I feel bitter just venting to You. But thanks for listening. Continue to speak to me through Your words and Your presence. May I come to know

You better.

Thanks. Have mercy on me, a sinner. I love You.

Mike

Mike, I invite you into my intimacy, into a loving relationship with Me, your God, savior, and lover. Accept My invitation—I long for you in love.

Thanks, Lord. You get me through. Have mercy on me, a sinner. I love You.

Mike

September 6, 1995

Mike, love yourself—I do.

Praise and more to You, O Holy God, for having made me in Your image. Wow.

Help me continue to learn to love. Help me realize that its ok to admit my imperfection. I'm a sinner in need of You. Accept me tonight, in my hopes and fears and love.

Have mercy on me, a sinner. Thanks. I love You.

Mike

September 7, 1995

Father, if it is Your will, take this cup of suffering from Me. Yet not My will but Your will be done.

Mike, learn from Me and follow Me in love and trust.

Lord,

Accept me tonight, resistant, tired, sick, sinful, and worried. Help me, Lord, I need You very much.

Thanks for helping me and being there for me and with me. Help me to be open to You.

Have mercy on me, a sinner. Thanks. I love You.

Mike

September 8, 1995

They crucified Him.

Mike, I want to be your personal savior. Let Me love you and save you for Myself.

Praise and thanks to You, O Most Holy Crucified One. Accept me and my anxiety and fear. Continue to have mercy on me, a sinner. Thanks. I love You.

Mike

September 9, 1995

Mike, I became sin for you to save and set you free for Me, My love.

Lord, receive me tonight, exhausted and anxious for rest. If it be Your will, grant me healing rest. Thanks. Accept me, anxious and worried and walking to my Lord. Have mercy on me, a sinner. Thanks. I love You.

Mike

September 10, 1995

Mike, take delight in Me.

Proclaim the reign of God by loving with My love, and heal your afflicted brothers and sisters.

Wow! Praise to You, O Holy God, for calling me. I'm an unworthy, sick, and sinful man. Grant me the grace to rejoice in You, to love with Your love. Accept me and my anxiety. Thanks. Have mercy on me, a sinner. I love You.

Mike

September 11, 1995

Mike, proclaim My reign, by yourself, for your life. Be Mine in love.

Lord, accept me tonight. Thanks. It's been a long, hard day. I need sleep. Have mercy on me, a sinner. Thanks. I love You.

Mike

September 12, 1995

Mike, proclaim the reign of God. Heal the afflicted by sharing My merciful love for you and them.

Lord, thanks for calling me. I'm sick, unworthy, anxious, and sinful, but accept me tonight. Thanks for having mercy on me, a sinner. I love You.

Mike

September 13, 1995

Mike, love yourself as I do.

Lord, thanks for Linda. I'm struggling tonight, but I have "good guilt." Forgive me for my resistance and for not leaving myself. Accept me tonight, exhausted and anxious, and continue to have mercy on me, a sinner. Thanks. I love You.

Mike.

September 14, 1995

Mike, Love yourself as I do. You are very loveable. On the cross, I died to set you free for Me.

Praise be to You, O Glorious Risen Crucified Savior, God. Thanks, thanks. Accept me tonight, exhausted and anxious and wanting to grow in Your love. And have mercy on me, a sinner. Thanks. I love You.

Mike

September 15, 1995

They crucified Him.

Mike, I died for you because I love you.

Lord, I am in awe. You, Glorious and Crucified God, died because You love me. Thanks. I want to cry, it feels so good and so sad. Accept me, anxious, sick, and sinful but falling in love with You, and have mercy on me, a sinner. Thanks. I love You.

Mike

September 16, 1995

They crucified Him.

Mike, I died for you because I love you and want you to be Mine.

Thanks, Lord. Accept me tonight, exhausted and anxious, and grant me rest if it is Your will. Thanks. I love You. Have mercy on me, a sinner.

Love, Mike

September 17, 1995

Love Me above all, and love others, and love yourself.

Lord, help me to love. I'm guilty of putting my anorexia before You. Forgive and accept me tonight, and continue to heal me and to reveal Yourself and Your love for me. Thanks. I love You.

Mike

September 18, 1995

Love yourself.

Lord, accept me tonight. I don't really like me. I'm too fat, and I'm anorexic. I've gone from 99 to 100. Fluids? I'm sick, too, Lord, sinful, sick, and anxious, but hopeful. You love me, so I have hope. Thanks. Have mercy on me, a sinner. I love You.

Mike

September 19, 1995 (4:30 AM)

Dear Lord,

Receive me tonight. I'm wide awake after four hours' sleep. There's a big party downstairs—crash, bang, yells—and I can't sleep. I'm upset and anxious, and I need sleep. I offer this time to You—maybe it's a time to get back in touch with the problems that are on my mind.

I'm awfully sick, Lord, enslaved by anorexia and sin. I'm a selfish and proud man, much in need of You, and despite all the pain, fatigue, guilt, and shame—it's like I'm camped out in the storm—I'm slowly beginning to get in touch with myself and with You.

Your love for me is awesome. Earlier tonight, a TV minister said "God made You my Lord, who didn't know sin, to be sin for me." In my place, You took on the effects, the pain, the guilt and shame and punishment that I deserved for my sins. Wow, that's how much You love me. It is awesome.

I'm starting to feel and believe in forgiveness by You, my Lord, and I'm even trying to forgive, to accept and love myself. It's beginning, inwardly, slowly. You are helping me break free of my cycle of guilt, shame, and anxiety. It's new, and at times even uncomfortable—ha!—as if, at times, I should feel like garbage because I am bad, and yet I don't.

I still need to be aware of my sinfulness and selfishness and to repent. It's hard to do in a healthy and humble way—not hating myself, but being honest—yet I *am* a sinner. I'm not perfect. But I am also a little icon made in Your divine image. My calling in life, to get in touch with that image, with the me You created in goodness and love, and to let this image be Your love and goodness, to be seen in my life by others—this calling means letting go of all the garbage that consumes me. This little icon, in me and in others, it's a beautiful and powerful wish and yet it is so real a goal. And You are with me, Lord, to help me through it. Thanks.

I'm not progressing much outwardly. I still want to lose weight, still want to be in control. I feel that others (Helen, Linda, etc.) might soon try to force me to gain weight, and I want to be ready—if I can lose a little, then I'll have more room to play with. But I am eating healthfully and nutritiously. I just need to eat more vegetables. I'm being too hard on myself, because in very small ways I am eating more, however slowly, and I'm scared of deviating for fear of losing control and gaining weight. It's scary, at times, because I can die for this, and yet I'm confident that You will see me through. Thanks.

That's all for now Lord. Thanks for listening. I'll try to go back to sleep. If it is Your will, grant me rest—if not, I offer You this day in my tiredness, knowing that I will catch up, because I am sleeping much better.

Thank You. Have mercy on me, a sinner. I love You.

Mike

September 19, 1995

Love yourself, Mike.

Lord, receive me tonight, exhausted and sinful. I'm so weak and needy, falling so far short of Your call to know Your love for me and others. Thanks for being there in so many ways Help me to love more. Thanks. Have mercy on me, a sinner. I love You.

Mike

September 20, 1995

They crucified Him.

Father, forgive them.

Mike, listen to Me and trust in Me and My love for you.

Praise and thanks to You, O Holy One, for dying for me. Accept me, anxious, sinful, and sick, and have mercy on me, a sinner. Thanks. I love You.

Mike

September 21, 1995, Christopher's Birthday

Rejoice, Mike! Healthy people don't need doctors, sick people do. I've come not to call the self-righteous but sinners.

Thanks, Lord, for calling me into Your mercy and love. Accept me, exhausted and anxious, and have mercy on my brother and on me, a sinner. Thanks. I love You.

Mike

September 22, 1995

They crucified Him.

Father, forgive them.

Mike, believe. Come to know Me. I suffered and died to free you from your sins for Me.

Praise be to You, O Most Glorious Crucified God, Savior and Lover. Thanks for the gift of Yourself and for calling me to intimacy. Have mercy on me, a sinner. Thanks. I love You.

Mike

September 24, 1995

The crowds came to Him, and He spoke to them about the reign of God.

Mike, listen to Me in love.

Praise be to You, O Holy Crucified Risen God—thanks! I had a great week after You helped me listen to You in love. Accept me tonight, sinful and sick, and continue to have mercy on me, a sinner. Thanks. I love You.

Mike

September 25, 1995

I will receive you, speak to you, and heal You, Mike, My beloved.

Glory to You, O Holy God and Savior. Thanks. I offer You me, anxious, worried, and exhausted, yet thankful that You are healing me and revealing Yourself to me. Have mercy on me, a sinner. Thanks. I love You.

Mike

September 26, 1995

Come to Me, My beloved. I will receive you, speak to you, heal you, and feed you.

Thanks, Lord for calling me to You—wow!—and for accepting me as I am. Receive me tonight, exhausted, anxious, sick, and sinful but grateful. Continue to have mercy on me, a sinner. I love You. Thanks.

Mike

September 27, 1995

Why don't you give them something to eat?

Mike, let Me feed you with Me, and then go and feed My people with love.

Praise, O Glorious God, Bread of Life. Thanks for forgiving me. Help me to revere Your body and blood, Your life and self. Thanks. Have mercy on me, a sinner. I love You.

Mike

September 28, 1995

Why don't you give them something to eat yourself?

Lord, I am hopeless without You. I want to grow, but I have nothing to give. Accept me tonight, and help me toward Your acceptance of me, despite my unacceptability, for You can work wonders. Receive me tonight, anxious, worried, and tired, and have mercy on my brother and on me, a sinner. Thanks. I love You.

Mike

September 29, 1995

They crucified Him.

They crucified Me for you. That is how precious you are to Me—I want you!

Lord, accept me tonight, exhausted and anxious. Thanks for dying for me—wow—thanks. Have mercy on my brother and on me, a sinner. I love You.

Mike

September 30,1995

They crucified Him.

Mike, I love you and want you so much that I died for you.

Thanks, Lord, Forgive me for being so self-centered and accept me tonight, anxious. Guide me to listen in fear and love for You. Thanks. Have mercy on me, a sinner. I love You.

Mike

Oct 1, 1995

I AM the Messiah, your personal God, lover, and savior—trust in Me.

Praise, O Holy One, crucified and risen and now with me to save me. Accept me and my fears and worries, and have mercy on me, a sinner. Thanks. I love You.

Mike

Oct 2, 1995

Mike, I AM the Messiah, moment by moment, and now.

Lord, thanks. Accept me tonight, and open me, anxious and worried. Accept me and my fears, and open me to receiving You as my messiah, now. Have mercy on my brother and on me, a sinner. Thanks. I love You.

Mike

Oct 3, 1995

I am your crucified and risen messiah, now! If you want to be My lover and follower, deny yourself, take up your cross, and follow in My steps of love and trust!

Dear Lord,

Thanks for four hours of sleep. I was tired, but now can't get back to sleep. But it's ok. You will take care of me

Maybe it's good that I'm up. I'm stressed and scared, facing choices, risks, and failure, unsure of myself and worried. I have to decide by Sunday on an out-of-town job. It would be easiest to stay here in Binghamton, secure and hoping to get another chance on the Civil Service List in four years. But is it a mistake to reject opportunity? By saying no now, I might be closing the door in the future. Help me to decide, Lord.

In New York City, the money, lack of family contact, and renting would not be worth it. I don't think it would. But maybe Willard . . . It would be challenging, scary, with no Mass, with a change of my routine—up every day at 5 to work at 8. It would be scary. Help me.

If I leave Binghamton, I take a new job where I risk ending up with nothing. If I get the job and blow it, the prospects are terrifying. And yet You have gotten me through so much in life. Lord, forgive me that my trust is so weak. Help me.

Perhaps I simply need to let go and listen. You will guide me if I let You, and You will give me what I need.

Thanks. I love You. Have mercy on me, a sinner

Love, Mike

Mike, who do you say I AM for you?

Lord, You are the messiah of God, my love and my savior. Thanks for helping me decide to take charge of my useless guilt. You have saved me once again. Continue to help, and to have mercy on me, a sinner. Thanks. I love You.

Mike

P.S. If it is Your will, help me to rest.

Oct 4, 1995

Mike, I AM with you now. I am your Messiah, and I will be with you wherever you go. Simply be open to Me. I love you.

Thanks, Lord. It's ok now. I don't know where I'm going, but it's ok. I'm confident that You will get me through. Thanks for being there for me in QT, Eucharist, in my family. And accept me tonight, anxious, sinful, but grateful. Thanks. I love You.

Mike

Oct 5, 1995

I am your messiah.

Thanks, Lord. Accept me tonight, a sinner, anxious, and grateful. Thanks. Have mercy on me, a sinner. I love You.

Mike

Oct 6, 1995

They crucified Him.

Mike, I took your place on the cross, suffering and dying to set you free for Me. Let Me love you—it's ok not to be perfect.

Thanks, Lord. accept me tonight, and forgive my broken, sinful failures. I'm disappointed and ashamed that I am too sick to pursue job opportunities. Forgive me for wasting my life and for being so sick and sinful and selfish. Have mercy on me, a sinner. Thanks. I love You.

Mike

Oct 7, 1995

They crucified Him.

Mike, I died for you. I love you just the way you are, and I want you to be Mine. It's ok if you are sick and sinful—I love you and want you. Believe.

Thanks, Lord. Accept me broken, sinful, anxious, and exhausted, but hopeful. If it is Your will, grant me rest. Thanks. Have mercy on me, a sinner. I love You.

Mike

Oct 8, 1995

I AM your God and messiah.

Praise! Thanks to You, O Holy One, for everything, for Yourself, my family, Father T, and my life. I offer You me tonight, grateful, anxious, sinful, and in love with You. Have mercy on me, a sinner. Thanks. I love You.

Mike

Oct 9, 1995

I AM your God and messiah, crucified and risen. I gave Myself totally for your care. I love you and want you.

Lord, accept me tonight, anxious and tired. Help me to live for You, Jesus, as Father T said today. And have mercy on me, a sinner. Thanks. I love You.

Mike

Oct 10, 1995

Mike, carry your cross with Me. Follow Me, for I AM with you every step of the way, and I love you. Rely on Me.

Thanks, Lord, Accept me tonight, anxious and sinful, and have mercy on me, a sinner. Thanks. I love You.

Mike

Oct 11, 1995

Follow in My steps, Mike. I AM with you.

Lord, accept me tonight, exhausted, sick, and anxious, yet thankful that You are with me and that I need You. Grant me rest if it is Your will. Thanks. Have mercy on me, a sinner. I love You.

Mike.

Oct 12, 1995

Mike, follow in My steps. Submit to My Father's will. In His will is your peace, joy, and salvation, for I AM with you.

Lord, accept me tonight, anxious and sick, and grant me rest if that is Your will. Help me, Lord, to follow as You did, and continue to have mercy on me, a sinner. Thanks. I love You.

Mike

Oct 13, 1995

They crucified Him.

Mike, I love and want you. Follow Me. Die to your selfish self.

Lord, accept me tonight, exhausted, anxious, sick, and sinful. Help me by granting me rest, if that is Your will, and continue to have mercy on me, a sinner. Thanks. I love You.

Mike

Oct 14, 1995

They crucified Him.

Mike, I love you so much. I died for you. Believe.

Thanks and praise to You, O Holy Savior. Accept me, broken, tired, sick, and sinful, but grateful for the mercy You have on us, especially my brother and me, a sinner. Grant me healing and rest if it is Your will. Thanks. I love You.

Mike.

Oct 15, 1995, Transfiguration

Listen to Me, Mike.

Lord, accept me tonight, tired, worried, guilty, anxious, and sinful. Help me let go of my selfish self and listen. Have mercy on me, a sinner. Thanks. I love You.

Mike

Oct 16, 1995

Mike, listen—I AM in you.

Lord, accept me. I am powerless, and You died to free me. Receive me, sinful and anxious, and grant me help in rest if that is Your will. Have mercy on me, a sinner. Thanks. I love You.

Mike

Oct 17, 1995

Mike, listen to Me in quiet time and with others.

Lord, accept me tonight, powerless, sinful, and anxious, yet grateful and in love with You. Help me to let go and listen in love. Have mercy on me, a sinner. Thanks. I love You.

Mike

Oct 18, 1995

Listen to Me in love. I want to reveal Myself to you in your heart.

Thanks, Lord. I'm sorry for being such a mixed-up person. Forgive me and heal me, Lord, and accept me, anxious, worried, sick, sinful and in love with You. Have mercy on me, a sinner. Thanks. I love You.

Mike

Oct 19, 1995

Listen to Me, Mike, and let go of your worries and guilt. I love you.

Lord, accept me, exhausted, sick, gassy, stomach hurting, and tired. Help me, if it is Your will, and grant me much-needed rest and the grace to learn to die to my selfish sinfulness and to live for Your faith, in and with You. Have mercy on me, a sinner. Thanks. I love You.

Mike.

Oct 20, 1995

They crucified Him.

Father, forgive them.

Mike, I died for you, taking on your sins so that you might be freed to live in love with Me.

Thanks, Lord. Accept me tonight, anxious, worried, and sinful. Grant me rest and help me if that is Your will. Thanks. Have mercy on me, a sinner. I love You.

Mike

Oct 21, 1995

Mike, My Father speaks also—listen to us.

This is My Son, My Beloved, listen to Him.

They crucified Him for you and all.

Lord, accept me, in awe of Your love, Blessed Holy One. Grant me continued healing rest, if it be Your will. Have mercy on me, a sinner. Thanks. I love You.

Mike

Oct 22, 1995

Listen to Me—I love and want you.

Mike, die to your sinful attachment and become detached and open to Me, dead to sin, and clean for My Father in Me. I AM your hope.

Lord, accept me, tired, anxious, and sinful. Grant me the grace to become detached from what is not Your will and to cling to Your Father's will as You did. If it is Your will, grant me continued healing and rest. Have mercy on me, a sinner. Thanks. I love You.

Mike

Oct 23, 1995

Listen to Me. I AM in you, here with you, now.

Thanks, Lord. Accept me, exhausted, anxious about my weight and health, and very sleepy. Grant me the grace to accept Your will and to continue to heal and rest. Have mercy on me, a sinner. Thanks. I love You.

Mike

Oct 24, 1995

I AM your God. I am with and in you and healing you. Believe and be in awe of My being.

Praise be to You, O Glorious One. Accept me anxious, sick, sinful, and in need of You. Have mercy on me, a sinner. Thanks. I love You.

Mike

Oct 25, 1995

Mike, I Am with you and in you. Marvel and be in awe at My presence.

Thanks and praise be to You, Most Holy One, Accept my anxiety, worries, sickness, and sinfulness, and continue to have mercy on me, a sinner. Thanks. I love You.

Mike

Oct 26, 1995

Marvel at My greatness. I AM in you and in your life.

Thanks, Lord. Help me to open up to Your acceptance of me. Have mercy on me, a sinner. Thanks. I love You.

Mike

Oct 27, 1995

They crucified Him.

I died for you. I AM with you, now.

Lord Jesus Christ, Son of God, have mercy on me, a sinner. Thanks. I love You.

Mike

Oct 28, 1995

They crucified Him.

Mike, I AM with you and in you and there for you. I died for you because I love you.

Lord, accept me, broken, scared, tired, and worried, wanting and not wanting to change. Let me receive my treatment for my anorexia, for my sinfulness, and be with me. I am falling in love with You. Have mercy on me, a sinner. Thanks. I love You.

Mike

Oct 29, 1995

Pay close attention to Me, Mike. I suffered and died to save you, and I want to save you now. Open up to Me.

Lord, accept me tonight, tired, sick, sinful, and anxious, and help me listen and open up to You. And continue to have mercy on me, a sinner. Thanks. I love You.

Mike.

Oct 30, 1995

Mike, be attentive to Me. You can't save yourself. I will redeem you and receive you to Myself in loving tenderness.

Thanks, Lord. I offer You me—broken, sinful, and anxious as I am. Continue to have mercy on me, a sinner. Thanks. I love You.

Mike

Oct 31, 1995

Mike, be humble before Me, your God, and you will meet Me in love.

Lord, thanks. I offer You me, broken and sinful. Have mercy on me, a sinner. Thanks. I love You.

Mike

Nov 1,, 1995 All Saints Day

The least among you is the greatest.

I want you to be humble before Me. You can't save yourself. But I want to, and I can, and I will if you will allow Me.

Lord, I offer You me—poor, broken, sick, sinful, and anxious. But in my poverty I am blessed—thanks. Have mercy on me, a sinner. I love You.

Mike

Nov 2, 1995

Come after Me.

Lord, I am an unfit follower. I want to follow, but I get distracted. I am sinful, sick, anorexic, and unworthy. Help me to let go of what separates us, and accept me. I offer You my life, Lord Jesus Christ, Savior and God. Have mercy on me, a sinner. Thanks. I love You.

Mike

Nov 3, 1995

They crucified Him.

Father, forgive them.

Mike, I accept you and forgive you. I want you to be mine—I love you very much. I died for you.

Lord, I feel like crying tonight. I'm broken, humble, sinful, and sick, and I am unworthy of Your gift of Yourself. I am so blessed by You. I am anxious, guilty, and ashamed, for I know that I let my sins block me from You, and it makes me sick and crazy. Have mercy on me, Holy God, for I am a sinner. Thanks. I love You.

Mike

Nov 4, 1995

They crucified Him.

Father, forgive them.

I am your savior.

Lord, accept me, sick, a sinner, broken, and tired. If it is Your will, grant me continued rest and healing. Have mercy on me, a sinner. Thanks. I love You.

Mike

Nov 5, 1995

Mike, I come for you, a sinner, daily. I AM with and in you. I AM your salvation.

Praise be to You, O Holy Savior. Receive me tonight, and forgive me for taking You for granted and being distracted. Continue to heal me, Lord, and grant me rest if that is Your will. Have mercy on me, a sinner. Thanks. I love You.

Mike

Nov 6, 1995

Mike, I called you, and I long for you to be Mine. Be a laborer for Me. Proclaim that My reign is here, now, with your life.

Thanks and praise to You, O Holy One. Accept me, anxious, sinful, and grateful in love with You, and if You will it, grant me continued healing and rest. Have mercy on me, a sinner. Thanks. I love You.

Mike

Nov 7, 1995

Mike, become like a child—trust, love, and be open. I want you and will reveal Myself to you.

Thanks, Lord. Accept me, exhausted, guilty, and sinful. Forgive me and grant me rest, if it is Your will. Have mercy on me, a sinner. Thanks. I love You.

Mike

Nov 8, 1995

Mike, you are blessed. I AM revealing Myself to you.

Praise be to You, O Holy One. Accept me tonight. Thanks for blessing me. Grant me continued rest and healing if that is Your will, and help me to be open to You. Have mercy on me, a sinner. Thanks. I love You.

Mike

Nov 9, 1995

Mike, you are anxious and worried about so much. Simply seek Me and listen.

Lord, accept me, broken and sinful. I need You. Receive me tonight, and have mercy on me, a sinner. Thanks. I love You.

Mike

Nov 10, 1995

They crucified Him.

Father, forgive them.

Mike, I love you. I died for you. I AM your savior, right now.

Thanks, Lord. Accept me, sick, stressed, and sinful. Grant me continued healing and rest, if that is Your will, and help me to be open to You. Have mercy on me, a sinner. Thanks. I love You.

Mike

Nov 11, 1995

They crucified Him.

Father, forgive them.

Mike, I love you. I forgive you now. Let Me heal you and save you.

Dear Lord,

Accept me tonight, hurting, sinful, and guilty. I feel awful and ashamed. I am so caught up in my sinfulness, my selfishness, my problems with anorexia and control. I put my family through so much, and I am so rigid and demanding. Forgive me, and have mercy on them.

Help me, Lord, to change—to begin anew and to experience Your forgiveness. Help me learn to change, to be less rigid and demanding and more flexible and agreeable. Thanks, Lord, for the opportunity to grow in Your love.

Forgive me and continue to heal me and grant me rest if it is Your will. Have mercy on me, a sinner. Thanks. I love You.

Mike

Nov 12, 1995

Mike, you worry about so much and are so anxious—let go and trust in ME. Be attentive to Me. That's all you need. I AM all you need.

Thanks, Lord. Accept me, sick, sinful, and anxious, and grant me healing and rest if that is Your will. Have mercy on me, a sinner. Thanks. I love You.

Mike

Nov 13, 1995

Father, hallowed be your Name.

Mike, pray in awe, reverence, longing, and humble love.

Lord, accept me tonight, exhausted, sinful, anxious, and sick. Grant me the grace to pray in loving awe, and continue healing my body and mind. Grant me this, if it is Your will, and help me to seek You and Your forgiveness and let go of all things. And have mercy on me, a sinner. Thanks. I love You.

Mike

Nov 14, 1995

Mike, let Me teach you to pray, live, and love in Me.

Lord, hallowed be Your name, Your kingdom come. Accept me tonight, worried about my foot, my health, and my sleep. I'm a sinner seeking what I want—grant me the grace to seek Your kingdom—in that, I will have life. Have mercy on me, a sinner. Thanks. I love You.

Mike

Nov 15, 1995

You can depend on Me, Mike.

Thanks, Lord. Accept me tonight, trusting that You'll give me my daily bread and Your life and who I need. Continue to have mercy on me, a sinner. Thanks. I love You.

Mike

Nov 16, 1995

With Me you shall want for nothing.

Grant me this day, Your daily bread, O Holy One. Accept me, sick, sinful, and anxious, and continue to have mercy on me, a sinner. Thanks. I love You.

Mike

Nov 17, 1995

They crucified Him.

Father, forgive them.

Mike, I died for you. I love you, and I am with you, and I AM all that you need.

Lord, accept me tonight, exhausted, anxious, sick, hurting, and sinful. I am worried about my ankles being infected and being unable to walk; about eating and gaining weight; about my butt and bleeding and gas; about my health, and Thanksgiving. I am guilty about my messed-up sleep and prayers and life—life alone can be too much at times. I'm scared that I am really sick, too sinful and mixed-up, and powerless—I can't make it on my own. My way doesn't work. But I am scared to change, to let go and turn myself over to Your loving care. Forgive me, Lord, and help me open up to You in my sinfulness, brokenness, and poverty. Thanks. Have mercy on me, a sinner. I love You.

Mike

Nov 18, 1995

They crucified Him.

I AM your savior.

Thanks, Lord. Accept me, thankful, sick, and sinful, and continue to be my savior. Have mercy on me, a sinner. Thanks. I love You.

Mike

Nov 19, 1995

Mike, ask, seek, and knock. Ask for the Holy Spirit, and He will come.

Lord, accept me tonight, anxious about my foot, my gas, my butt, my sleep. Receive me, a sinner, and grant me the gift of opening up to You, O Holy God, Holy Spirit. Have mercy on me, a sinner. Thanks. I love You.

Mike

Nov 20, 1995

Let Me show Myself with you by giving you My spirit.

Thanks, Lord. I love You. Have mercy on me, a sinner.

Love, Mike.

Nov 21, 1995

Call on Me, and I'll save you. Trust me. I love you.

Thanks, Lord. Accept me, tired, anxious, and sinful, but grateful, and continue to have mercy on me, a sinner. I love You.

Mike

Nov 22, 1995

Mike, I AM your God. I want to share Myself with you, intimately and in love, through the Holy Spirit. Be thankful, rejoice, and be humble!

Thanks, Lord. Accept me, a sinner, sick, anxious, and grateful, and continue to have mercy on me. Thanks. I love You.

Mike

Nov 23, 1995

Trust in Me and have no fear. I am with you and in you. I love you, and I AM your savior.

Thanks, Lord. Have mercy on me, a sinner. I love You.

Mike

Nov 24, 1995

They crucified Him.

I AM your personal God, you savior, and I love you and I AM with you.

Thanks, Lord. Have mercy on me, a sinner. I love You.

Mike

Nov 25, 1995

They crucified Him.

Mike, I AM with you in your suffering. I love you.

Thanks, Lord. Have mercy on me, a sinner. I love You.

Mike

Nov 26, 1995

Be happy, for you are blessed to hear My word.

Thanks, Lord. Have mercy on me, a sinner. I love You.

Mike

Nov 27, 1995

Be happy to hear My word, for I AM your God, who loves you very much. Believe and trust.

Lord, accept me tonight. Thanks for blessing me with Yourself, for revealing Yourself to me, even in my sickness and pain. Continue to have mercy on me, a sinner. Thanks. I love You.

Mike

Nov 28, 1995

Mike, your happiness is in listening to Me and keeping My word in love.

Lord, help me to let go and focus on You and Your love, for that is all I need. Accept me tonight, sinful and sick, and continue to have mercy on me, a sinner. Thanks. I love You.

Mike

Nov 29, 1995

Be happy, listen to Me, and keep living in My word and in My love for you. Don't be afraid. I AM with you, my beloved one.

Thanks, Lord. Receive me, tired, sinful, and sick, and have mercy on me, a sinner. I love You.

Mike

Nov 30, 1995

Father, forgive them.

Mike, I forgive you and love you. It's ok to need Me—it's your greatest strength. For your brokenness, be open and dependent on Me, and on My love.

Lord, thanks. Help me to accept Your offer. Have mercy on me, a sinner. Thanks. I love You.

Mike

December 1, 1995

Father, forgive them.

Call on Me. I want to save you, My beloved, and I will.

Thanks. Accept me tonight. Have mercy on me, a sinner. Thanks, Lord. I love You.

Mike

December 2, 1995

They crucified Him.

Call on Me. I want to save you, and I will. I love you.

Thanks, Lord. Have mercy on me, a sinner. I love You.

Mike

December 3, 1995

Rejoice in Me. Don't be afraid. I AM with you.

Thanks, Lord. Have mercy on me, a sinner. I love You.

Mike

December 4, 1995

Rejoice. Don't be afraid. You have found favor with Me. I AM with you and in you, My beloved.

Thanks, Lord. Have mercy on me, a sinner. I love You.

Mike

December 5, 1995

Mike, Learn to trust in Me and in My will. I love you, and I want what's best for you. Let go of controlling and open up to loving. I'll take good care of you.

Thanks, Lord. You got me through the day today. Grant me rest, if it is Your will. Thanks. Have mercy on me, a sinner. I love You.

Mike

December 6, 1995

Don't worry. Seek Me and My will. Love me in all things. I'll take care of the rest. I will give you very good care. Trust Me.

Lord, I am blessed to be called to be Your handmaid. Let Your will be done through me. Thanks, Lord. Have mercy on me, a sinner. I love You.

Mike

December 7, 1995

My mercy is on those who fear Me.

Lord, thanks. Have mercy on me, a sinner. I love You.

Mike

December 8, 1995

They crucified Him.

Let Me love you, Mike.

Lord, thanks. Have mercy on me, a sinner. I love You.

Mike

December 9, 1995

I love you, Mike.

Lord, thanks. Have mercy on me, a sinner. I love You.

Mike

December 10, 1995

Courage—I AM with you. Don't fear.

Lord, thanks. Have mercy on me, a sinner. I love You.

Mike

December 11, 1995

Don't be afraid—nothing can separate you from Me and My love for you.

Lord, thanks. Have mercy on me, a sinner. I love You.

Mike

December 12, 1995

Don't fear—I AM with you. I AM your God and savior.

Lord, thanks. Have mercy on me, a sinner. I love You.

Mike

December 13, 1995

I AM God's Son. I AM with you and will continue to save you.

Lord, thanks. Have mercy on me, a sinner. I love You.

Mike

December 14, 1995

Let Me be your savior, Mike. I love you and want you.

Lord, thanks. Have mercy on me, a sinner. I love You.

Mike

December 15, 1995

They crucified Him.

I died for you because I love you. I want you to be Mine.

Lord, thanks. Have mercy on me, a sinner. I love You.

Mike

December 16, 1995

I love you. Let Me save you. Give yourself to Me in love.

Lord, thanks. Have mercy on me, a sinner. I love You.

Mike

December 17, 1995

I AM with you. Don't be afraid. Trust Me.

Lord, thanks. Have mercy on me, a sinner. I love You.

Mike

December 18, 1995

It is I—don't be afraid. I'll save you.

Lord, thanks. Have mercy on me, a sinner. I love You.

Mike

December 19, 1995

I AM God, and I AM saving you from your sins—rejoice!

Lord, thanks. Have mercy on me, a sinner. I love You.

Mike

December 20, 1995

Rejoice, for I will save you, My beloved one.

Lord, thanks. Have mercy on me, a sinner. I love You.

Mike

December 21, 1995

Rejoice! I AM your savior.

Lord, thanks. Have mercy on me, a sinner. I love You.

Mike

December 22, 1995

They crucified Him.

I died for you. I love you. I AM with you now, to save you. Surrender yourself in trust, to let Me love you and to let Me love through you.

Lord, thanks. Have mercy on me, a sinner. I love You.

Mike

December 23, 1995

Rejoice! I AM your crucified savior, your God and lover, My beloved one.

Lord, thanks. Have mercy on me, a sinner. I love You.

Mike

December 24, 1995

I AM God. I AM with you. I AM your savior.

Lord, thanks. Have mercy on me, a sinner. I love You.

Mike

December 25, 1995

Rejoice! I AM with you and among you with love, My beloved.

Lord, thanks. Have mercy on me, a sinner. I love You.

Mike

December 26, 1995

I AM with you.

Lord, thanks. Have mercy on me, a sinner. I love You.

Mike

December 27, 1995

I love you. I AM with you always.

Lord, thanks. Have mercy on me, a sinner. I love You.

Mike

December 28, 1995

I AM in you and in love with you.

Lord, thanks. Have mercy on me, a sinner. I love You.

Mike

December 29, 1995

Father, forgive them.

I forgive you. Believe. Rejoice.

Lord, thanks. Have mercy on me, a sinner. I love You.

Mike

December 30, 1995

I love you. Let Me love you, and let me love through you.

Lord, thanks. Have mercy on me, a sinner. I love You.

Mike

December 31, 1995

I AM with you, now and always, and I love you.

Lord, thanks. Have mercy on me, a sinner. I love You.

Mike

Dialogue 4: 1996

January 1, 1996

I AM your savior—Jesus—I will save you. I love you.

You shall name him Jesus (Yahweh saves).

Thanks, Lord. Have mercy on me, a sinner. I love You.

Mike

January 2, 1996

Fear Me and rejoice in Me—I AM in and with you. I AM your God and savior.

January 3, 1996

Call on Me in fear, and rejoice in Me, for I have mercy on you and I AM saving you.

January 4, 1996

Don't be afraid. Listen to Me. I AM your savior and God. I AM with you and in you. I love you immensely. Rejoice!

January 5, 1996

The Word became flesh.

They crucified Him.

Mike, I came into this world for you, to save you. Let Me be your savior and God. Let Me share My life with you.

January 6, 1996

I came to die for you. I came to save you because I love you and want to share My life with you.

January 7, 1996, Epiphany

Prostrate your love before Me, and do Me loving homage.

January 8, 1996, Baptism

I AM God's Son. Be still and know Me in love.

January 9, 1996

I AM here and with you. Reform your life and believe in Me. Have My life, and have it abundantly, with Me and in Me.

Wow, Lord, it is Your birthday.

January 10, 1996

Remember, you are dust, and unto dust you shall return. I AM your life, your love. I AM all that is important.

January 11, 1996

Be reformed, be renewed, turn from sin and open up to Me, your savior and God.

January 12, 1996

They crucified Him.

I forgive you—let me love you, Mike.

January 13, 1996

Take and eat this. It is My body. I died for you and gave you Me because I love and want you— take care of yourself, Mike. I love you.

January 14, 1996

Take this and eat it—this is My body.

I AM with you—be aware of Me. I love you—be good to yourself.

Take care of your love.

January 15, 1996

Take care of your heart.

January 16, 1996

Take this and eat it. It is My body.

I AM your God, and I feed you with Me—this is the Bread of Life. There is no greater love than this, that I gave Myself up for you. Feed on Me, and I will remain in you and with you.

Take care of your love—I love you.

Dear Lord,

Accept me today, scared and hopeful. I saw Helen last night. I've lost weight, and I'm sick and weak. It's possible to drop dead from heart failure, though it's not likely. But it scares me. I don't want to die.

I'm afraid of change. I need to take care of my heart and not lose weight. Hospital visits and death are consequences of my failure to take care of myself.

I'm scared, and I call on You, My Holy God, to help me take care of my heart by feeding me a little more every day.

Thanks. Have mercy on me, a sinner. I love You.

Mike

January 17, 1996

Let me feed and nourish you with Me. Let Me live in and with and through you. I died and gave Myself for you, that you might have life. Take care of your heart.

Take and drink My blood, which I shed for the forgiveness of your sins. I paid for your sins because I love you and want you to be Mine. Accept My forgiveness and My love.

Thanks. Have mercy on me, a sinner. I love You.

Mike

January 18, 1996

I paid for your sins on the cross because I love you.

January 19, 1996

I died for you on the cross because I love you.

Jan, 20 1996

Come to know Me—I AM with you always. Let Me help you take care of yourself.

January 21, 1996

Happy the man that doesn't lose his faith in Me.

I died for you. Take this and eat this, My body.

I care about you. I want you, and I want you to take care of yourself.

January 22, 1996

Your will be done.

Mike, I AM with you in your sorrow.

January 23, 1996

I experienced great distress and sorrow, and I made it. Let Me be your strength in living My Father's will.

January 24, 1996

I will be your strength in your desire to give yourself up to My Father's will. Let Me help you.

January 25, 1996

Call on Me. I AM your strength and your life. Trust Me.

January 26, 1996

I love you immensely, personally, and passionately. I died for you because I want you to be Mine. Let Me love you and reveal Myself to you.

January 27, 1996

Be still and know that I AM your God. I love you.

January 28, 1996

Blest are you who are poor in spirit. I AM with you, Mike. In acknowledging your poverty, brokenness, and sinfulness, and the needs that you bring to Me, you will be more open to Me.

January 30, 1996

I AM there for you and your brother, with all the hurting and the poor.

January 31, 1996

Know you that I AM with you.

February 1, 1996

I shed My blood for you.

February 2, 1996

I died for you.

February 5, 1996

Blessed are you who are poor in spirit—in your broken, sinful poverty, you can be rich in Me. I love you.

February 6, 1996

Hail, King of the Jews!

I became poor and broken for you because I love you.

Blessed are you who are poor in spirit. You are open to My kingdom, to My living in and with and through you.

February 7, 1996

In your neediness and poverty, come to know Me and My limitless love for you.

February 8, 1996

I AM your God and lover—come to know me in silence. Be in awe at My glory and majesty, for I AM Lord.

February 9, 1996

They crucified Him, then kept watch over Him.

I love you just as you are, Mike, My broken little one.

February 10, 1996

I want to be with you and to have you know Me.

February 11, 1996

You are blest in your brokenness and poverty, through which you can come to know Me. Take time and slow down, for I love you.

February 12, 1996

Listen to Me in your need, in your brokenness and poverty.

February 13, 1996

They led Him out to be crucified.

I AM with you to help you carry your cross.

February 14, 1996

Follow Me as I carry My cross in obedience, self-sacrifice, and limitless love.

February 15, 1996

I AM with you to help you carry your cross—rely on Me.

February 16, 1996

They crucified Him, then kept watch over Him.

Come to know Me, in loving silence.

February 17, 1996

Be open to Me and My healing love, in loving silence.

February 19, 1996

Believe in Me, and come to know Me and My love for you, in silent adoration.

February 20, 1996

I love you—be open to Me.

February 21, 1996

Be still and silent in My love. I AM in you.

February 22, 1996

Mike, pray with Me.

My Father, not My will but Yours be done.

I will help you.

February 23, 1996

Dear Lord,

Help me to be more accepting, forgiving, and loving of others and myself. I'm hurting, guilty, scared, and demoralized.

Saturday, Bob and Colleen really hit me hard. They were very critical, and lots of it was true. I feel incompetent in counseling, like I'm hurting people by being a coward, by being sad and rejected. I feel guilty. They didn't acknowledge my apologies, and now I'm scared. I have to go back to work, but can't go back to how it was. I don't want to be close to them, but I'm afraid to upset them for fear that they will get me.

Help me let go and open up to Your guiding love—I don't know what to expect and how to handle our friendships, which all seem broken. I feel like I lost a part of my life. It hurts, and I'm sad and afraid to go further. But I can't turn back the clock. Help me to trust You, and thank You for helping me if I let You.

Thanks. I love You. Have mercy on us and on me, a sinner.

Love, Mike

Don't be afraid. I AM with you and will help you, my precious little broken one.   .

February 24, 1996

Be in My loving presence. Let me love you. You don't need to do anything—just be you.

February 25, 1996

I call you to know Me in love. You shall do homage to Me alone and adore Me. I AM your God, savior, and lover.

February 26, 1996

Adore Me in love, my beloved, and know Me in love.

February 27, 1996

I want to share Myself and My life with you.

February 28, 1996

Sit and be silent before Me. It's ok. I'll help you take care of your cares. I love you.

March 1, 1996

I died for you because I love you as you are.

March 2, 1996

Be still before Me and come to know Me.

March 3, 1996

I AM God's only Son. Don't be afraid. I AM with you and in you, and I love you—listen.

March 4, 1996

Listen and don't be afraid. I love you.

March 5, 1996

My grace is all you need. Call on Me in humble love.

March 6, 1996

I AM in love with you, and I AM with you.

March 7, 1996

Let Me save you. I love you and want you.

March 8, 1996

Call on Me and I will save you.

March 10, 1996

My food is to do the will of Him who sent Me.

March 11, 1996

I love you.

March 12, 1995

I AM your savior.

March 13, 1996

Let Me save you and be your savior.

March 14, 1996

I forgive you and want to save you—let Me save you. I love you.

March 15, 1996

Remember me, Jesus.

I AM with you now in the midst of your suffering—let Me be your savior.

March 16, 1996

I love you. Believe and be still. Be aware. I AM in you, and nothing can stop Me from loving you.

March 17, 1996

Believe in Me and My limitless love for you.

March 18, 1996

Listen.

March 19, 1996

Call on Me often and listen.

March 20, 1996

I AM with you in your suffering.

March 21, 1996

I AM with you in your suffering.

March 23, 1996

Repent, and be open to Me.

March 24, 1996

I AM your life.

March 25, 1996

I thirst for you.

March 27, 1996

I AM in and with you in your suffering.

April 1, 1996

Accept My forgiveness, My love, and My life.

April 3, 1996

Salvation is My gift to you.

April 4, 1996

Just be with Me, My beloved.

April 5, 1996, Good Friday

When they had crucified Him, they sat down and kept watch over Him, claiming this man was the Son of God.

April 6, 1996

I died loving you. I died for you.

April 7, 1996, Easter

Peace—don't be afraid. I AM alive for you and with you.

April 8, 1996

Peace. I forgive you and love you immensely, and I want you to be Mine.

April 9, 1996

Peace—don't be afraid.

April 10, 1996

Full authority has been given to Me. I AM your God and savior. I AM with you always. I love you and want you to be Mine.

April 12, 1996

I was crucified for you because I love you and want you to be Mine.

April 13, 1996

I AM God's Son. I died for you because I love you.

April 14, 1996

Find life in Me. Call on Me. I AM your life.

April 15, 1996

Thank You for giving me Your life.

April 16, 1996

I AM your life.

April 17, 1996

What you ask in My name I will do.

Lord, have mercy on my brother.

April 19, 1996

I love you as you are.

April 20, 1996

I gave My life for you and now give my life to you.

April 21, 1996

How slow you are to believe and come to know Me. Listen and let Me reveal Myself to you in love, My beloved.

April 22, 1996

Know that I AM with you always.

April 24, 1996

Rest in Me. Unburden your love to Me. Be detached from all things and rely on Me for I AM all-powerful and all-loving. I AM with you always.

April 24, 1996

Dear Lord,

It is one year now since I got sick. thanks for all Your help hanging in there, and for loving me so much and revealing Yourself to me and helping me with the pain. I am such an unworthy sinner.

I'm depressed and sad tonight, struggling and angry I went down to 96, but I'm now at 98, though I've probably lost muscle. I struggle daily with fatigue and with gas pain wrenching through my insides. I'm preoccupied with passing gas and relieving the pressure. I'm sad and pitiful, and it's my own fault. I'm often too sick and tired to be of use to anyone, let alone to be Your servant, distracted as I am by pain and obsessive thoughts. I'm so sick, sinful, and selfish, and I have trouble even bleeding and sleeping.

Lord, I have wasted and ruined the life You have given me. I say I am sorry so often that it's sickening, because I don't want really to change. I don't want to deal with my brokenness. It's scary and disgusting and depressing.

Lord, I offer You me in my brokenness, the good, bad, ugly, sick and sinful person that I am. Forgive me and accept me in my brokenness. I am unworthy of You and Your love, but help me to accept Your forgiveness and love and to believe that all You want me to do is to believe in You, listen, and love.

Thanks. Have mercy on me, a sinner. I love You.

Mike

April 28, 1996

I came so that you could have life to the fullest.

April 29, 1996

I AM the good shepherd. I lay down My life for you—come to know Me.

May 1, 1996

Return to Me.

May 2, 1996

Come to know Me. I love you and want you for Myself.

May 25, 1996

Dear Lord,

Help. I'm struggling. I gained weight, from 96 to 99 I think. Maybe I didn't. I can't go to the bathroom, and now I'm depressed that I'm still struggling to diet and lose. I can't pray—I'm too sinful and sick I'm caught up in myself, in worries and fears about training, lunch, sleep, QT, Mass, vacation, not getting to 96—oh, I'm upset, angry, and sad. I need You. I can't make it without You. Help me, Lord.

Thanks. I love You.

Mike

Jun 15, 1996

Father, forgive them.

Mike, I forgive you and love you, and I want you to take care of yourself. Trust in Me and My love for you.

Lord,

Accept me, broken, sick, sinful, and hurting with anorexia, I still don't weigh 98, and I feel fat. I'm obsessed, driven by vanity and distracted. Forgive me, Lord, for putting my dietary problems on You.

I offer You me today, Lord. I suffer, physically, from pain and exhaustion, and it's my fault. I've wasted what You gave me, and I'm unwilling to get treatment. I'm too sick, it's too frightening. Forgive me for being scared, weak, and selfish. Forgive me too for not being there for others, like Bob, Alice, and my family, friends, and clients.

Lord, I am handicapped by my sickness. Help me accept and love myself as I am, as You love me, and help me move on, relying on Your grace. Help me forgive myself.

Thanks. I love You.

Mike.

Accept My unconditional, passionate, limitless love for you, as you are now, despite your unacceptability.

Jun 16, 1996

Fear Me and nothing else. Call on Me and stop worrying. I will take care of you.

Jun 27, 1996

Be humble before Me. Realize your poverty, and seek detachment from all that is not Me.

Lord,

Receive me tonight. It's 2:30 a.m. I slept well, but I'm up now and stressed Benadril and cider caused me anxiety. Please help me to unwind and get some sleep. Thanks.

Lord, I'm in denial, minimizing the seriousness of my sickness. I'm depressed, and I can't seem to lose. I'm stuck at 99 and bummed out—I want to weigh 96. Sick, isn't it? And deep inside, I hurt. I know that my obsessive thoughts and lifestyle are killing me—physically, emotionally, and spiritually. Being so preoccupied with sickness, so very distracted, I am a failure, Lord. I am unable and unwilling to detach from this thing, this way of life, which keeps me from being open to You in love.

Forgive me Lord and have mercy on me, a sinner. Thanks. I love You.

Mike

July 4, 1996

Its 5:00 p.m. and a cool, rainy day. The rain has stopped, and sounds and smells of the 4th of July 4th are minimal.

This has been a retreat day on vacation. I'm just sitting here smoking after finishing two pieces of toast. I'm tired and numb, and a candle is burning in front of the crucifix—the symbol of the retreat and God's passionate love for his people, including me.

It's been a slow, quiet, pray-filled day, not a bad one—bland but calm. My quiet time has been deep. Usually I'm so rushed, tired, and bloated from gas that pain and cramps disrupt my time with my Lord. Now, I sit here alone, knowing what I should reflect on but not knowing how to begin.

During spiritual direction on Monday, Fr. T challenged me to love myself. It seems simple, but it's not. Rationally I can say that God made me in His image, that I reflect Him and His glory in a unique way. And I know I'm not really a bad person, but I don't feel all that good, either—I feel kind of gray. Yes, a part me is loving, loyal, dedicated, caring, compassionate, giving, generous, empathic, and kind. But at the same time, I am haunted by the me no one knows, the broken me, who is sick, sinful, weak, proud, guilt-ridden, vain, lazy, selfish, cruel, jealous, envious, and destructive.

I am a sinner, and yes, I believe God is my personal savior. He gives me joy and comfort in my sorrow. But I really haven't accepted myself. Throughout my life I've tried to deny myself—drinking, working, anorexia. I've hurt my family, friends, and many others, in addition to coming close to killing myself. I'm not suicidal—but I am self-abusive. I'm hard on myself—obsessed with dieting, with losing weight to feel good. And I'm so worn out and weak from this. The specialist said my progression has added thirty years to my body. And she's right—I'm 34 yet I feel 64 physically. Most days, I'm plagued by fatigue, hunger, exhaustion, and pain. And anorexia is a 24-hour job—every night is broken by trips to the bathroom to relieve my bladder.

I'm living a nightmare—at times, I'm living in Hell. I really do suffer—and yes, I know that I have done this to myself. I don't think I could so cruel to anyone else. I punish myself every day, and I don't let up a bit.

Deep down, I'm also disgusted and terrified about my sexuality. I can't believe anyone could love the whole and real me. I'm too ugly and disgusting. It's sad.

I'd like to finish this retreat and say that I'm beginning to love God, others, and myself, but perhaps I can't say that yet. I guess I could say that I'm beginning to get to know and care about myself. I'm not totally bad. I'm just a broken person who wants to love and be loved.

Lord Jesus Christ, Son of God, have mercy on me, a sinner.

Jul 21, 1996

You cannot serve two masters.

Dear Lord,

I am defeated. I've lost the fight. I'm destroying myself trying to serve two masters, You and anorexia. I am powerless. I feel sad and guilty that my response to You is so poor and broken. But I'm caught up in vanity, weight loss, and self-image. I am a hopeless sinner, not able or willing to change.

I almost got sick last night. I'm so weak, Lord. On my own, I'll self-destruct. I'm sick, obsessed, and sinful. My weight has gone from 100 to 101, or probably less due to digestive and bladder problems, and people see me as a skeleton, yet I feel fat, ugly, disgusting, and sinful. It's too much.

As bad as I feel about this, I do feel some hope and peace and joy because it's Sunday, the day we recall Your rising from death. You overcame defeat on Good Friday, Lord. You were crucified, taking on my sins and those of all humankind and loving us unto death. Lord, You are with me always in my self-inflicted Hell, and deep inside myself, I know You. I know that new life is possible because You rose in triumph of love, and as broken, poor, and sinful as I am, I know in some way that You and Your love for me are more powerful than my illness and sinfulness.

Today, I offer You me, and I ask that You help me begin my life. I am responding to You the best way I can, and I trust You will lead, guide, and help me. Thanks. I love You.

Have mercy on me, a sinner.

Love, Mike

July 23, 1996

My love for you is great, Michael. I will rescue you.

Lord, its 3:30 a.m. For the first time in a long while, I can't sleep. I'm stressed about losing minute amounts of weight and fighting to lose more. It's crazy, but it's where I am—stressed and anxious.

I went to my boss's birthday party—afraid of food, partying, and socializing, but I went for You—and I found out today from her significant other that I'm special to her. I want to be there, but I'm scared.

It's the same with Gene P. He wants to have lunch or coffee. I'm afraid. Lord, help me. I feel that You will guide me right, and it seems You want me to love. My priority is spending time with people, but right now I'm not healthy enough to eat normal food. I would only get sick. Still, help me to reach out to others and eat as well as I can, sticking to my regimen so I don't get sick. It's OK to just have coffee—I just need to eat in private. A healthy diet can save my life, and it isn't important to eat just to impress others with being normal. I am not, after all. Help me to accept my limits and reach out in love instead of hiding. I can rely on You.

Thanks. I love You. Have mercy on me, a sinner.

Mike

Jul 26, 1996

Dear Lord,

Tonight I recalled how You suffered and died on the cross for me and for all of us, because You love us so much that You willingly died and took our sins, so that we could be one in Your love.

Lord, I'm so weak, sinful, and unworthy—obsessed with my anorexia, depressed, eating less but still unable to lose weight. I feel fat, I'm in pain a lot, and my insides hurt. During prayer, I'm distracted. My relationships with my brothers and sisters are diminished by my physical, mental, and spiritual exhaustion. Lord, I'm defeated and broken, unable to make it on my own. I need Your help—save me. Forgive me for my stubbornness and pride, and help me submit to You in love.

Thanks. I love You. Have mercy on me, a sinner.

Love, Mike

Aug 1, 1996

Lord, it's 3 a.m., and I am sick. I was constipated, now I have diarrhea after too much prune juice.

I can't get back to sleep for anxiety. I feel broken and worried. I am at war with myself. Anorexia is driving me mad, and I'm getting very sick physically, emotionally, and spiritually. I'm smoking too heavily. I can't breath, I have pleurisy—lots of pain—and food gets stuck. I suffer all day and night. I'm broken and defeated, and I can't take it anymore. I don't know what to do.

I'm afraid. Perhaps it's a goal, though—the pain makes me preoccupied with change. As You know, I've struggled with horrible daily gas pain—drinking a quart and a half of skim milk in the morning is insane, my stomach can't handle it, yet I'm stuck with it because I'm sick and anorexic and the milk is protein rich and keeps me alive. The gas, though, destroys my peace of mind during prayer. I want to make a change. Help me, Lord, and guide me. I'm sick and scared. I don't want to die—or to continue to suffer or gain weight. Help me, Lord. I am a sinner. I need You.

Thanks. I love You.

Mike.

Aug 11, 1996

Good morning, Lord.

Thanks for the good sleep (10 p.m. to 9:30 a.m.). I've been exhausted, from anorexia, pleurisy, and gas. I'm sore, I have trouble breathing, and I'm depressed—I can't seem to lose weight; I'm stuck at 102—I'm obsessed, angry, and sad. I actually did lose a few—I was stuck at 104 to 105—so I can lose.

I'm sorry—I know this is not Your will. I can't be happy until I'm under 100, back in my comfort zone. It's going to kill me, but I'll actually feel better. Help me, Lord. I'm struggling. I want to pray, love, and live simply—help.

Forgive me. I'm sinful and sick. I need You. Thanks for loving me.

Have mercy on me, a sinner.

Love, Mike

Sep 2, 1996

Jesus, remember me when you enter into Your kingdom.

Let Me solemnly assure you, this day you will be with Me.

Mike, I AM with you now in your brokenness, and I long for you to be Mine—now in your suffering, and later in Paradise. Be open to Me.

Lord,

Today I am a broken, sick, and sinful man, unworthy of You and Your love. Forgive me. I have wasted and ruined much of my life, and I am still ruining it. As an anorexic, I'm caught up in myself, obsessed and often closed to You and others. Forgive me Lord, and help me open up a little more to You and others. O Crucified God, let me come to know You and Your love and to have Your love for others, as St. Francis did.

Have mercy on me, a sinner. Thanks. I love You.

Mike

Dialogue 5: 1996–1999

Sep 9, 1996

Dear Lord,

I come to You today sick, weak, and sinful. I have pleurisy and gas pain and breathing pain. My diet isn't working—the milk is causing me too much gas and pain. I'm broken. I called in sick to work, but I feel guilty. My anorexia and health problems are hurting my job performance. I also don't want to go to the staff party—I'm not ready to even try to eat something normal. Help. Forgive me.

Varying my routine isn't working. I've just been angry and depressed and disgusted at my attempts to lose weight. I left my comfort zone, gained, and got depressed. Now I've lost a little, but nowhere near enough. I want to get under 100 to feel good. I'm sick and insane. Lord, I want to try something new—tuna fish instead of milk—but I'm scared. If it works, I believe I can feel better about myself and my life. It should improve my time with You, too, so often broken up by gas pain, and my work and my personal life should benefit. Living in continuous pain has been too much. I'm really hurting, and I need and want to change—my job and my spiritual, emotional, and physical health depend on it. Help—help—help. I can't make it on my own.

Have mercy on me, a sinner. Thanks. I love You.

Mike

November 27, 1996, Thanksgiving

Jesus, have mercy on me, a sinner.

Your faith has been your salvation.

Dear Lord,

It's 2:30 a.m., and I'm up, anxious and awake. I slept well. I'm nervous, but I have been feeling better, sleeping well, and in less pain. The bleeding has stopped, and my prayer is deeper. Thanks for blessing me with faith, life-giving and life-saving faith in You, O Holy One. Thanks for family, health, and work.

I'm sick still, and anxious about losing weight. I want to keep changing my diet for the better and to lose, not gain, to get into my comfort zone. I was so scared tonight, Lord. Last year I blew it and was depressed for more than three-quarters of the year.

Have mercy on me, Lord. I'm sick and sinful, and I offer You myself tonight. Help me to call on You and rely on You and You alone. On my own, I'm stuck in a cycle of insanity.

Thanks, thanks, thanks Lord, for loving, forgiving, and dying for me and for all of us.

Love, Mike

December 21, 1996

Dear Lord,

Thanks. It's 2 a.m. I slept well, but I'm anxious. Help me to get some more good rest.

What a day—thanks for getting me through it and home safe and alive! I went to the nutrition counselor on Friday, but she was out. I started bleeding, and I thought it was hemorrhoids, so I went to a doctor without an appointment. They took me in because I was bleeding, and they made me lie down. I couldn't even move. They called an ambulance. I had internal bleeding—they feared I was hemorrhaging. I was terrified—was I dying? Would I have to be hospitalized? I almost broke down. At the ER, the doctor thought I had a bleeding ulcer from taking too much Advil (14+ per night) to ease my stomach, chest, and back pain, which were caused by my muscle weakness, gas, coughing, and anorexia. I'm destroying my body, Lord. Thanks for getting me home. I can't make it without You, and I don't want to. Help me to trust in You. Help me to stay out of the hospital and to serve You with my whole heart and love.

Thanks for having mercy on me, a sinner.

Love, Mike

February 5, 1997

I love you, and I washed away your sins with My own blood.

Dear Lord,

Accept me tonight, exhausted, guilty, stressed, sick, and sinful. Thanks. Physically, I'm slowly getting better. You are healing me. I'm still awfully sick. Please continue to heal and save me. I need You to save me.

I am selfish, proud, self-righteous, judgmental, vain, unforgiving, envious, obsessive, and sinful. I'm also broken, physically, emotionally, spiritually. Forgive me Lord. Help me accept Your forgiveness and Your grace—help me accept Your life into the brokenness that I am so that I can be loving and forgiving like You. During Your Passion, through scourging and beating and crucifixion, You kept loving and forgiving. Lord, help me to love and forgive. I'm so weak, selfish, and sinful, and I can't do it without Your help.

Help me to accept Your forgiveness, and help me forgive others, especially my co-workers who hurt me today, and myself. I'm terribly hard on myself—help me to love myself and You and others.

Thanks. I love You. Have mercy on me, a sinner.

Love, Mike.

I forgive you and I love you—be forgiven, healed, and loved by Me.

March 20, 1997

Father, let it be as You, not I, would have it.

Dear Lord,

Receive me tonight, exhausted, sick, guilty, sinful, and broken. I'm so self-centered, vain, judgmental, and fearful. I've made myself very sick and weak. I've hurt myself in my relationships to You and others, being as sick as I am—all day and all night suffering and struggling. I feel like a hopeless failure.

Lord, You gave me so much, and I'm so closed to You and I reject so much. I'm so sinful for what You gave me—Yourself, my life, my family, friends and faith—and I've wasted it all. Forgive me for being selfish, jealous, and proud and for not being open to You and the help You have given me.

Lord, I offer You my broken sinfulness. I'm sorry for what I have done. Have mercy on me, a sinner. Thanks. I love You.

Mike

May 17, 1997, Pentecost

Trust Me and know that I AM with you always.

Lord, help. I'm hurting—anxious, tired, worried, and depressed. My butt is bleeding, and I'm in pain. Help me, Lord. Save me. Have mercy on me, a sinner. Thanks. I love You.

Mike

May 25, 1997, Trinity

Know that I AM with you, and come to know Me more and more.

Lord,

Receive me today. Thanks for this day of retreat and for calling me in love to know You more and more. Thanks for the gift of You, O Holy Son of God, who gave Your life out of love. How unworthy I am, so sick and sinful. I want to know You better and to go out and make disciples for You, Lord, but I'm so weak, so sick, and so sinful. I block You and others out with my sinfulness and anorexia. I'm too tired and selfish to be open to You and Your power to save me—forgive me, Lord. Thanks for healing me, saving me, and loving me. Help me respond in loving surrender and trust.

Lord, I offer You me tonight for those who do not know You—may You live and love through me, an unworthy, sick, and sinful servant.

Lord, I offer You my sufferings for my brother. He is hurting, he needs You, and only You can save him. O Lord, have mercy on him. Have mercy on us all. Have mercy on me, a sinner.

I love You. Thanks.

Mike

Jul 30, 1997

Courage, it is I. Do not be afraid, for there are no limits to My power to save.

Mike, trust me. I AM with you. I will save you if you will let Me. I AM the savior of all—trust Me and My love and power to save.

Dear Lord,

It's 3:30 a.m. Thanks for helping me sleep and for waking me now.

I feel like crying. Yesterday I turned in my boss for what I believe was unfair treatment of my co-worker. I am not happy I had to turn her in. I like her a lot, but I couldn't sit there and watch people get hurt. I tried speaking to her first, but it didn't do much good. I didn't want to hurt her, but maybe, hopefully, some hurt and help will be an opportunity for her to grow. I know that many of the hurts in own life have helped me grow. But I feel bad because she'll be in a lot of pain, and I know she cares a lot about me.

I want to cry. I'd like to tell her I'm sorry. I'm scared because I don't know where this will go—selfishly, I'm scared of losing my own job—I have financial cares, and I really like working with people. I'm afraid of going back to work to face our bosses—scared too that I didn't do the right thing, or didn't handle it the right way—scared too because she can hurt me in return. She's my boss and knows that I'm anorexic. I hope she doesn't choose to use that against me. I'm vulnerable. I know that it was a risk to tell her that, but I felt it was worth talking. I still do, because getting help saved my life. I hope she will get help too.

It's kind of funny, looking back—it's true that there are no limits to Your power to save. You get me and all of us through things. Help me to trust that You know what's best and to rely on Your grace to love. Have mercy on her, and on me in my adolescence, and on my family, and on us all. Help me to deal with my fear and sadness in healthy ways. Help me to grow more dependent on You.

Thanks for loving me and being with me and dying to save me. Have mercy on me, a sinner. Thanks. I love You.

Mike

Aug 31, 1997, Sunday Speaker Meeting, Binghamton Phelps Hall, 7:00 p.m.

I felt very nervous going to the meeting. It's been 13 years, and I am a recovering person who has been greatly blessed by God with the grace to live sober. I want to keep my working lie totally separate from my personal life, so I feared seeing clients and self-disclosure. I was relieved not to find any clients at the meeting. I was still nervous sitting down, but I felt welcomed. I felt like I belonged.

Early in the meeting, I was easily distracted. Members were reading and talking, and there were lots of echoes. One person commented that was glad to go to another room for small group discussions because of the poor acoustics of the old classroom we were in. I was glad to stay in the room, though, and I was able to get focused. As we circled around the discussion table, I felt welcomed and safe all over again. Then envy kicked in, and I was scared to take a place. What should I say, I worried, when it was my turn to speak.

But being attentive and open to the other speakers gave me peace. People were sharing the third step, "We made a decision to turn our lives and our wills over to the care of God." It was powerful to listen to again, after all these years. I'm not drinking, but in a lot of ways I am a dry drunk. I'm still plagued by the problems that led me to drinking. Life is good but hard, because the inner me is still very hurt and broken, and all too often looking for peace and healing in the wrong places. My life is still insane and unmanageable at times. But listening and pardoning gave me a feeling of hope and happiness. I still feel far short of the daily process of turning myself over to God's care and will, and I often get discouraged. I have many worries and cares that I seek to control. Listening gave me peace. Three members related how it had helped them experience the "care" part of the step ("God cares very much about me"), and described the peace that came with turning oneself over to the care of a loving God. It won't shield us from pain and suffering, but trust is the answer. I don't have to worry, because God's will is for me to trust Him to give me the help I need. With that, I can make it through the things that overwhelm me.

Sep 1, 1997

Going to my second meeting after years without was good. I was much more relaxed. Turning my worries over to God's care helped me immensely. I am generally very nervous and self-conscious in new places, but giving in again made me feel welcomed, like I belonged there, and relieved that I wouldn't have to speak.

During the meeting, former clients sporadically stopped to say hi, that it was great to see me, and shook my hand. Here I was no longer a counselor, just another human working on recovery. I felt connected and safe. The speaker, a man I know, really surprised me. After years of recovery, he went back out, and he's back on track again—he compared himself to a train. He reinforced the impotence of "rooms"—that is, AA fellowship.

As the meeting closed, we made a large circle, and I was humbled to be a part of something bigger then myself. We spoke the Lord's Prayer, and afterwards a former client shared his growth and hope with me. I needed that, because I've been in a rut lately.

Exiting the room, I felt nervous and in awe of the fellowship. People gathered outside to smoke and be together. I moved slowly beyond them and began my journey home, privileged to have elt the power of the fellowship even though I wasn't yet an active member of it. I left feeling hopeful.

Recovery works, and so does fellowship. Driving home, I couldn't help wondering if it might be good to be involved. Where I am today, though, I don't know if it would be the right thing to do. Maybe someday.

Sitting here now, at 4 p.m. on Labor Day, I'm preparing to go back for eleven days without a break. I'm thankful that I can go back after having received something to share. Not that I'll speak at length of this experience—but I hope that it will remain in the memories I take back to the DAC, and I hope to be able to pass it on.

Sep 5, 1997

Lord,

I do believe. Help my unbelief.

Today was day one of training. Thanks for getting me through, Lord, and accept me tonight. We learned about alcoholism as a disease, about obsession, compulsion, and sickness. I feel hope because I admit that I have a sickness, and You have granted me faith in Your power to save me. Help me to believe and trust and surrender more.

I'm so sick, enslaved by anorexia, fatigue, poor sleep, mental exhaustion, chronic pain, guilt, shame, sadness, bleeding, and gas. I offer myself to You tonight, Lord, You who suffered and died on the cross in my place (and in everyone's place) to defeat evil, sin, sickness, and death. You and Your love conquered all.

Have mercy on me, a sinner. Thanks. I love You.

Mike

Sep 12, 1997

Lord,

I went to Al-Anon on Wednesday. It was powerful. The third step was the topic, for the second time. It was only my second discussion meeting in fourteen years. I guess that You are trying to tell me something.

I'm finally beginning, little by little, to turn my life and will and worries over to Your care. I'm finding that I don't need to be enslaved to sick, worried, self-centered thinking. Thanks, Lord, for healing, freeing, and loving me so much, to the point of death on the cross. May I become a message of Your healing love.

Thanks. I love You.

Mike

Sep 13, 1997

Lord,

I'm powerless over my brokenness and sinfulness. My life's a mess. I believe that You love me and want to save me. Help me turn myself, my life, and my will over to Your loving care.

Thanks. I love You.

Mike

Sep 14, 1997, Triumph of the Cross

Lord, I do have faith. Help the little faith I do have.

Lord,

Accept me tonight. Help me turn my life and will and worries over to You and Your care and love, and to rely on You. Help me make changes to my diet without getting sick and bleeding. Help me at work. Help me to trust.

Thanks. I love You.

Mike.

October 18, 1997

Mike, the bread that I give you is Me, My flesh for the life of the world. I AM with you always. I AM your life. Let Me love you, live in and with and through you.

Dear Lord,

Thanks for loving me so much that You died for me and give Yourself to me daily. Help me to be more open to You and to depend on You. I can't make it on my own. I'm very sick, physically, emotionally, and spiritually. I'm a weak, selfish, sinful, and broken man.

Thanks for dying for me and reaching out to me in love daily. Help me to be more open to You in the moment. Forgive me for being so selfish and worrisome.

Thanks for revealing Yourself to me in silence and in others, especially in the man who asked me for a smoke tonight. I didn't want to be bothered and was scared he would hurt me, but all he wanted was to talk and be accepted—homeless, living at VOA, a misfit like myself, looking for You. In him, I saw Your goodness. I saw him looking for You and for love and acceptance. Help me give myself as You did.

Thanks. Have mercy on me, a sinner. I love You.

Mike

October 26, 1997

Jesus, have pity on me.

Your faith has saved you.

Mike, it's ok. Your faith in Me will save you. Trust in Me.

Jesus,

Help me to trust You and to take care of myself by facing my fears. I can't do it on my own. I'm overwhelmed and stressed out. I can't sleep, I'm nervous, I'm worried, I'm obsessed with the fear of change and guilty about how I have hurt my family. Help me, Lord. I'm sick. I don't want to change, but I fear getting sick, losing my job, and going into the hospital or dying. I can't make it without You. Help me.

Thanks. I love You.

Mike

November 5, 1997

Have pity on me Lord. Your faith in me is saving me.

I AM your God, and I AM with you. Give thanks to Me, for I AM good and My love for you is everlasting.

Lord,

Thanks, and forgive me for being so selfish and weak and sinful and sick. Thanks for loving me and being with me in my pain and emptiness. Have mercy on me, a sinner.

Thanks. I love You.

Mike

January 4, 1998

Jesus, have pity on me.

Your faith has saved you.

Mike, continue to call on Me through your suffering, and I'll continue to save you. Know that I love you very much. I died for you.

January 7, 1998

Jesus, Son of David, have mercy on me.

Your faith has saved you and will save you—trust Me.

Good morning, Lord.

Thanks for a new day and some sleep last night. I offer You my tiredness and suffering today and hope to sleep better tonight.

I'm really overwhelmed. I don't know what's causing my sleeping problems—probably anxiety and depression, on top of not spending a good hour with You every day, and of course smoking too much. Help me make small changes and offer my worries and cares to You.

I'm upset because I don't want to take medication for sleep or anxiety and depression. I feel my mental state for prayers would be diminished, and that is very important to me. Drugs would put a block between You and me, and the very thought makes me feel like a failure.

My anorexia has caused great hurt to me, my family, my job, and my relationship with You. Now I'm scared and nervous because I don't know what to do. Guide me, Lord. Help me give in to Your will.

Thanks. I love You.

Mike

P.S. Lord, I'll work on dealing with my stress and feelings this week, I'll stick with Rx 1 + 1, and I'll be open to therapy for depression and anxiety if that is what it takes. Guide me, Lord. I offer You my sickness and suffering, and I hope for Your help.

January 11, 1998

Mike, I AM your God, your personal Lord and savior, and I love you and want you to be Mine. I want to heal you and live with and through you.

Lord,

Thanks and praise to You. I love You and want to give You myself. Thanks for healing me. Continue to heal me as You choose to. Help me be open to Your way and Your will, and teach me to be more loving and more like You. I offer You my anxiety and fears about my health, anorexia, sleeping, family, and work. I trust that You will be with me to help me.

Thanks. I love You. Have mercy on me, a sinner.

Love, Mike

January 19, 1998

Lord, have pity on me.

Your faith in Me has saved you, is saving you, and will continue to save you. Believe in Me and My love for you. Let Me be your savior.

Dear Lord,

Thanks for being with me in my suffering, anorexia, and insomnia.

Help me, Lord. I'm scared. I can't sleep. Help me to get help through my doctor. He wants to give me a prescription for depression and insomnia. I've fought it, but now I think I have no choice—my physical and emotional health depend on sleep, and so does my job.

My pride is broken, Lord. I've failed, I'm powerless, I can't sleep due to anxiety and anorexia. My body is wasting away, and insomnia is part of it. My only hope is medicine, sleep, and making very small changes to stop losing weight. I have to stabilize and even gain a little by Easter. But it's overwhelming. My only hope is You, and Your grace, because I can't handle this on my own. I'm truly powerless, overwhelmed by fear of insomnia, bleeding, weight gain, and depression. I'm almost suicidal and I fear going crazy, losing my job, and being hospitalized.

Help me make little changes, slowly, with medicine and a little more food every day. I don't think I can make it, though. Only with You, Lord, I've failed and can't make it on my own. Help me surrender. I'm scared of being depressed on medication, and I feel guilty now that my life depends on it. This insanity has been ruining my life for fifteen years. I offer it to You, tonight, and I call on You for healing so that Your power and glory may be shown through me. May I love and serve You. Thanks for loving me and for calling me in my selfishness and giving me more love. Help me to sleep a lot more tonight. I will start getting better with medication and nutrition.

Thanks. I love You.

Mike

Mike, it's ok. I want you to start reaching away from yourself. Stop beating yourself up.

February 16, 1998

Take this and eat it. It is My body.

Dear Lord,

Thanks for loving me and all people so much that You sacrificed Yourself for us and our sins. You have given Yourself for me, O Most Holy One. Forgive me for not being open to receiving You and letting You live in, with, and through me. I'm so unworthy and yet so blessed.

Lord, You are my only hope. I'm mentally, physically, and spiritually sick and sinful. I've put my pride, selfishness, fears, and vanity before You and my fellow men, and I have limited my ability to be Yours—You who call me to be Yours in love. Forgive me, Lord and, help me let go of my will and be open to Your love.

This Lent, may I die to selfishness and be open to receiving You, O Most Holy Son of God. All praise be to You, Lamb of God, O Saving Victor who sacrificed Yourself, dying on the cross to set us free.

Thanks. I love You. Have mercy on me, a sinner.

Love, Mike

October 6, 1998

Mike, put your trust in Me. I love you, and I want you to be mine. I want to save you so that you can serve Me and be a witness to My love.

Dear Lord,

Thanks for the pain and sickness and suffering that have led me to You and Your love.

Forgive me, Lord, for my resistance to You, for abusing my body, and for my impurity. I'm broken and sinful, and I need You as my savior. I love You, Lord—help me to trust and be open to Your call.

I don't know what to do. I'm uncertain about my future. I don't want to change—I really love working with my brothers and sisters, and I fear losing my job. Help me, Lord, to be open to Your guidance. Help me to trust that if I seek Your will, things will work out and be a glorious sign of Your love and saving power.

Thanks. I love You. Have mercy on me, a sinner.

Love, Mike

November 11, 1998

Mike, call on My Name and I will save you. I want to forgive, save, and heal you, and to be with you and love you. Please let Me.

Dear Lord,

Thanks for calling me. I'm so sinful, selfish, proud, vain, jealous, untrusting, and unworthy of You and Your love. It's overwhelming to me that You could really love me and want me to be Yours.

Tonight, I'm having trouble sleeping. I'm all stressed out. The new doctor will keep me on a prescription for my problems. I told her about myself today. I'm a pretty sick person. I could see her looking at me like a very sick and dying person. My family's worried, too. It hurts to see my dad's face and hear his voice.

Lord, forgive me. So many people care about me and love me, and I'm wasting away. Sometimes I feel it would be better to be dead, if it meant I could be with You and not have to suffer and be so sick anymore.

Lord, teach me how to suffer and love. I offer You the insanity of my anorexia. Help me, Lord. Forgive me and save me, love me and heal me, Lord. Accept me as Yours.

Thanks. I love You.

Mike.

December 20, 1998

Mike, I love you. I washed away your sins with My own blood.

I AM your God, your lover, and your savior. I forgive you and love you, and I want you to be Mine.

Dear Lord,

Thanks for forgiving me, for loving me as I am, uniquely me, and for dying for me.

Help me accept and experience Your love and forgiveness, personally and uniquely to me, and to see the uniqueness of Your love and goodness to me and others. Help me to love like You do and let go of my fears, jealousy, and resentment. Help me to be as accepting and loving of myself and others as You are.

I'm stressed with holidays, the cold weather, the coming new year, and fear of job loss or change. Help me to trust in You and rely on You.

I love You.

Mike

February 11, 1999.

They crucified Me for you and each person.

.

Dialogue 6: 2000

April 17, 2000

Mike, it's ok. I AM with you. You are My intimate friend.

You shall love Me with your whole being, love others, and love yourself. —Mark 12

Take this, it is My body.

Father, let it be as You would have it.

Then they crucified Him.

Know that I AM with you always.

Jesus,

Help. I'm scared. I don't know what to do. Fear, job loss, insecurity, vacation, scheduling, Mass, sleep, digestion, health—I am sad and afraid, and I don't know what to do. Help me to stop, pray, and listen to You. Help me to love You and let You guide me. Help me to trust in You. Thanks for five years of recovery and six years of sobriety and sixteen years of human services. Help me to love.

Thanks. I love You.

Mike

Lord Jesus Christ, Son of God, have mercy on me, a sinner.

I want you to be all Mine.

March 18, 2000

Know that I AM with you always. —Matthew

Dear God,

It's 3:15 a.m., and I am up and can't sleep. I'm very anxious. I got scary news Friday at 4:30 p.m. I may lose my job as a drug counselor at DAC. I'm upset. I love my job, I love working with people, I love counseling. I don't know what will happen or what my options are, but I'm glad I at least won't be jobless. It's just major change that scares me—schedule changes, having to dress up, trying to get to Mass; fear of exhaustion, constipation, insomnia, missing Mass, being sick, not being able to counsel. It's upsetting.

I offer You me tonight. I want to trust You and put this in Your hands. You've never failed me. I trust in Your love, Your will, and Your way for me.

Thanks. I love You.

Mike

April 19, 2000

Lord Jesus Christ, Son of God, Have mercy on me, a sinner.

I'm sad, worried, and afraid. What is going to happen to my job, my career? Use me as a missionary warrior in Binghamton. Thanks for the options I've received: CDSU/case manager, jail counselor, DSS case worker, DSS examiner, BC Office of Employment and Training. Help me to love like You.

Thanks, Jesus. I love You.

Mike

Michael's Letters to His Mother: 2001–2003

January 14, 2001

Dear Mom,

Just a quick thank you for all you do and are for me. God has truly blessed us all, but especially with you for my mom. You teach me much, and your love and support bring me closer to Jesus, because the love you have for us all in your loving heart comes from Jesus. Thanks too for great Christmases and birthdays. You always make me feel like a million dollars. I hope your back gets better. Sorry I've been on your case about things.

Enclosed are a rosary ring and a prayer card. I'd like to ask you a birthday favor. Sit in your chair once a day, close your eyes, and breath slowly in and out, realizing Jesus is in you and with you. Don't think any thoughts or images. Just be aware of Him. As you breath in, slowly pray "Lord Jesus Christ, Son of God." As you breathe out, pray "Have mercy on me." Do ten of these—use the rosary ring to count. Simply be aware of Jesus, Who is with you now, and call on His Name. Try it for a week. He wants you to know Him more intimately.

Thanks, Mom. You're in my prayers. May God bless you. Stay close to Jesus. He loves you very, very much.

Love, your son, Mike.

May 9, 2001

Dear Mom,

Happy Mother's Day!

Its 7:30. I had a good night's rest, and I'm happy to be alive this morning. Thanks for being my mom. Thanks for teaching me to play baseball!

I bet you never thought I'd be saying that to you. But seriously, I listened to Colleen and Kelly talking about raising their children and how important it is to teach kids to play the game of baseball, which is life. They're worried because children today don't seem to know the rules of the game, and it's not the kids' fault. They often have nobody to show them how to play.

Throughout my childhood and up to the present, you have showed me how to play and live the game of life, and I want to thank you because today I'm happier than anyone I know. I like playing the game of "baseball," or life, and I learned how from you and Dad and my brothers. Mom, you're a great and wise coach. Thanks for helping me learn the many rules of the game:

- *Respect*. I still call Mr. and Mrs. Fertig "Mr. and Mrs. Fertig." I still write to relatives and visit them. I still say "please" and "thank you," hold doors for women and men, respect old people, listen when someone is talking, and take turns.

- *Teamwork*. And other valuable social skills. When we were kids, you taught my brothers and me how to play together: to share with others (maybe that's why I like Catholic Relief Services so much), to play fair, and not to gossip or talk unkindly. If you could teach the rest of the world those things, I think half the world's problems could be eliminated.

- *Apologizing.* I make up and shake hands rather than holding a grudge if I have a disagreement. "Make up with your brothers" and "I'm sorry" are the two essential expressions for our relationships with others and God. Beneath these words is the essential attitude, which is love. As my mom, you taught me how important love is. It determines whether we win or lose the game of life.

Jesus says, "Love one another" and "There is no greater love than to lay down your life for your friends." Mom, you have shown me God's love through your own love for me and my brothers. You've followed Jesus's example by laying down your life for "your friends": your husband, sons, relatives, and neighbors, and for sick people, lonely people, and forgotten people by baking cakes, sending cards, and visiting. These are the little rules of the game that lead to happiness: to share and care and give.

When I was hurting and down, you once asked me "Why did God make you?" and I knew the answer because of your love. God made us to know, love, and serve him, to be happy and to be eternally in Heaven with Him. And a few months ago, you told Christopher and me "We are all God's children." Too often I forget this. If all people tried to play the game with that rule in mind, maybe the other half of our problems would be solved—hatred, violence, war, abortion, loneliness, addiction, greed, selfishness, and starvation.

Thanks for teaching me, showing me, and coaching me. I don't have my own family, but I try daily to show and teach others, like my clients, what you taught and showed me. Big, tough guys coming out of prison respond quite well to the number one rule, "Love one another." Actually, everybody I know likes it when I play by the rules.

Mom, I'm running out of time. I need to shower and pray so I'll be ready to go out into the world and play the game of life, happy to be alive. There are a lot of things I've forgotten to thank you for. But thanks all the same. You're still my coach, and I am still playing on God's team. We can't worry about losing with Him as the owner of the team. Thanks for being my mom and loving me.

May God bless you as you keep teaching and loving, being yourself and being my Mom. I love you a lot, and Jesus loves you much, much more. Stay close to Him. You are in my prayers and my heart.

Love, your son, Mike.

May 28, 2001

Dear Mom,

Happy Memorial Tuesday. I had a great night's rest. I feel like a million bucks. I certainly have problems, but I'm happier than anyone I know. You know why? Dad told me years ago, when I

was drinking, that I can be as happy or unhappy as I want. And you told me that God made me to
know, love, and serve Him. That's my happiness. Jesus is in love with us, with you and me, and
I'm in love with Jesus and His brothers and sisters. I'm sad though that there is so much
suffering in our world, some people starving to death physically while others starve spiritually.
But the only thing we can do is love. That's life's secret. Jesus taught love and you have lived it
and given it to me. Thanks, Mom. I love you.

Memorial Day is a time to remember the victims of war and famine. We always used to get
together at Grandmother's—I'm homesick for my family—but sadly, we're spread out and too
busy now. But that's OK—what counts is that we love each other. That's what Grandmother and
Dad's family and Aunt Gert and your family taught me. I'm happy to be a part of our family, and
I feel sad for people like Bob who don't have one.

My retreat was awesome. I feel like crying because I want to share it with others—quiet time
spent in love with Jesus and wanting to love others as He does.

Jesus said, "As the Father has sent me, so I send you," and then He breathed on them and said,
"Receive the Holy Spirit."

"Come Holy God, come Holy Spirit, enkindle in our hearts the fire of your love. Glory to you
Holy God, now and forever."

I guess that's all for now. I'm happy to be on my way to Mass to receive Jesus and then to come
home to you, Dad, and Christopher. How happy I am. We even got more rain. People at work
can't understand why I like rain so much. Rain is an important part of life, and it makes me
happy—it cleans things and help things grow. It kind of reminds me of my relationship with
Jesus. Daily, I need Him to cleanse me of my sins and help me grow in His love.

Try to spend some quiet time with Jesus today. He's in love with you. You're in my prayers.
Thanks for giving me love and a home and a family to come home to. May God bless you.

Love, your son, Mike.

November 16, 2001

Dear Mom,

Happy 65th birthday! I hope this is a good year for you. Our family are all blessed by God to
have you—you don't how much you mean to me.

Jesus asks only one thing of us: "Love one another." I'm happier than anyone I know—people at
work think that I am crazy because I'm so happy and hopeful, always trying to see the good in
others. I'm falling in love with Jesus and His brothers and sisters. You showed me His love and
helped me to love him, others, and myself. Thanks. You said we are all God's children, and the
more I see this, the more precious life is. because each one of us is a special and beautiful child
of God, whom Jesus loves so much that He died for us.

You also told me, when I was hurting with my alcoholism, that God made me to know, love, and serve Him. That's the secret to life. I'm sad when I see so many people suffering, and I want to do all I can to help them know Jesus and His love for them. I fall very short, but He forgives me and helps me keep loving more and more like Him.

I apologize for all I've put you through, and I want you to know how much it means to me to have you and Dad and Rob, Kathy, Christopher, and George. You are my family, and you always make me feel like a king returning home from a long trip.

I had a great visit with Helen today. She sees me making a lot of progress—eating regular bread instead of light bread is a major accomplishment for someone like me. I even had an extra slice of bread today, and I've never done that before. Your love, support, and prayers are paying off for me. Thanks a million, Mom! God's healing me a lot, and I'm happy to be me today. As Popeye the Sailor used to say, "I am what I am, and that's all that I am." Today can say that like Popeye, I'm happy to be me, despite my sinfulness and shortcomings, because God is helping me love Him, others, and myself more and more.

Thanks again. Happy early Turkey Day from a real live turkey: "Gobble, gobble!" And happy birthday, Mom. I love you! You're in my prayers. Stay close to Jesus and Mary His Mother— Jesus and His Mother love you very, very much.

Love, your son, Mike.

May 9, 2003

Dear Mom,

Happy Mother's Day. Thanks for being my mom and loving me. God has blessed me by giving me you for my mom. You're always there for me, and you make me feel like a king when I am at the house.

I wish weekends didn't go by so fast. The greatest thing a person can do in life is love. You have shown me this, that love is the secret to life—without it we are miserable. I'm happier than anyone I know because I'm falling in love with Jesus and my brothers and sisters. I'm blessed to be at jail and feel God calling me to a deeper love, and that's a reason I'm doing retreats. He is my lover and is letting me get to know Him more personally. He is in love with us and longs for us to let Him love us and know Him more intimately.

Mom, thanks for loving me on sunny and cloudy days, through ups and downs and in-betweens. Your love has helped me give up drinking and learn to live with my eating problem. I'm sorry for you, because I imagine it's not easy being my mom because of all my problems. But that's what love is all about—loving unconditionally—you never stop loving, and I hope I can do the same with my life.

Thanks, Mom. I love you. Happy Mother's Day! You're in my prayers. May God bless you and reveal Himself to you more intimately.

Love, your son, Mike

Michael's Final Struggles with Anorexia: 2007

June 9, 2007

When I woke up this morning, I didn't know where I was. I was happy to be alive and well rested. I thanked God. But I grew anxious thinking about having a smoke and going home and back to work.

I'm upset because I have to comply with therapy or I can't get a doctor's statement to go back to work. I have to comply in order to get my medicine. It sucks being dependent. I wish I could have a bowel movement without taking a laxative. I wish I could sleep without medication.

I don't want to gain weight, but I know I have to to stay alive. I can gain some without being fat, though, and if I gain too much, I can get rid of it when I am free.

I'm hopeful. I'm sad for my family. I'm embarrassed because I'm such a mess-up. I'm happy because God is good. And I'm thankful for the people here, who are so kind. I'm blessed.

I want to love and be loved. I want to make my family happy. I enjoy drinking energy juice and apple juice. Tube feeding (through the nose) is bittersweet, the wheelchair is too. I'm embarrassed to take up so much of the workers' time and worry that others will resent me. It's weird, but writing about me seems so selfish. I'm getting in touch with a lot of things.

The opposite of anorexia is eating healthy and being happy and sociable—not caring about calories and weight, and being free to eat, live, work, and sleep in peace. It's being able to live without sadness, accepting my illness and my need for God and others.

- Do you want to die?

- Do you want to change?

- Will you change?

- What do you want?

- Will you let go of anorexia, or at least try?

- Why do you hang on to it, when it hurts your family?

- Why do you cheat on yourself?

- Why do you still want to lose weight?

- Why do you want to stay at an unhealthy weight?

- Isn't anorexia a sick way of getting down, using others and feeling my sinful self?

- What does God want?

- Gain a little weight, stay alive, and don't die.

- Realize that you don't have to gain a lot.

- Know that you can take it off if you want, but you don't have to.

- Pray to the Lord for strength.

- The best way to be today is in the hospital.

- Talk to others.

- I am hopeful that I can stomach tube feeding. This is very good.

June 10, 2007

I don't want to die. I don't like this. I want to be able to have a bowel movement. I might need to use laxatives safely. I'm ok with that. It's scary and upsetting, but if I honestly try to change, I will be ok. I don't want to gain weight, and I know that as soon as I'm free, I can play the game and gain some. It's insane, but it's ok, because I'm starting to accept the idea of gaining a few pounds

I wish I could go away where no one knows me and start again. Embarrassment, guilt, shame, and sin suffocate me. I live to eat just enough to survive without gaining weight. I'm in a dangerous place. I'm being tube fed. Maybe they think I'm going to die. I want to help, but I can't smoke, and I want to get the hell out of here. I need to comply with the MD just to go back to work, so I'm forced. Otherwise I have no job, no meds, and I'll end up dead.

I cling so tightly to thinness. I've got to gain 5 to 10 pounds. That would still leave me thin. I need to be healthier for my family—they desire me, and it's selfish to cut them out of my life because I choose to be sick. I'll try. It's ok to make a little progress.

June 11, 2007

Forgive me for cruelly hurting my family.

Help me to change.

Help me to love.

Help me to let go, even if only a little.

I'm scared about BMs, cigs, sleep, weight, work, and playing the game. And being a liar.

Help is on the way in this place. It's ok to be sick and imperfect. Tonight, I'm happy. I didn't leave—no medicine is Hell. And if I do leave, I'll lose my job, so I have to stay and get Dr. T to write a letter saying I'm ok to work.

I'm in a fight for my family, job, clients, and life. I'm scared, but I'm ok right now.

June 14, 2007

I'm scared. The doctor said he wants me to go to rehab and isn't willing to do paperwork for me to return to work. I'm scared, tired, constipated, and nervous. I'm angry that I have so little control. It's not fair that after all my hard work in the past week, he can deny me my livelihood. I'm embarrassed, humiliated, and guilt-ridden for what I put my family through. I'm messed up and a loser. I'm angry that I got put in the hospital against my will, even though it may save my life.

Help me love, help me live, help me listen, and help me go home and back to work.

July 9, 2007

Dear Mom and Dad,

I hope all is well. I miss you both a lot and look forward to your phone calls. It reminds me of Staten Island. I miss Saturdays and Sundays with you. Thanks for all your support, kindness, love, and acceptance. You both mean the world to me.

I'm sorry to have put you guys through some really rough times. I hope I can make some of that up by getting closer to you. I'm slowly getting better. God is good, and He is helping me change. The people here are very special, both the clients and the staff. Sad but true, there's too much suffering and not enough Jesus. He is our only hope. I'm blessed very much because you have given me life's greatest gift—faith in Jesus and His love. I'm so sad that so many don't know Him.

I'm happier than anyone I know because of Jesus, because of His love, your love, and my ability to love others. Thanks for teaching me to care, love, serve, and listen. I'm working on eating more every day. God is helping me, and I have hope.

Two new girls just came in, one bulimic and one anorexic. The first seemed very scared. I said hi and helped her take her dishes to the window to be washed after dinner. The other girls are really reaching out to her, and she seems less scared now. She's even smiling. I keep all the girls' names in my notebook and try to pray for them during the meals.

I guess that's about all for now. I miss you guys and look forward to coming home. You're in my prayers. May God bless you both.

Love, your son, Mike

Remembrances

Michael's Final Years

On returning home from the rehab, Mike went back to work. His assignment changed, and he started at the Department of Social Services (DSS), where he would interview clients applying for welfare. He was hospitalize again when his weight dropped off. When he was discharged, his doctor suggested that he live with someone so he could better gauge his eating behavior.

Michael came home stayed with us for about a year. It was a heartwarming experience for all of us. Many evenings, I would sit in our rec room watching talk shows while he worked on crossword puzzles, and he got me hooked on sudoko. He said it was good for my mind. He also started attending AA meeting, and he looked forward to going almost daily.

Twice during that time, we had to rush him to the hospital to build him back up again, and he was eventually forced to retire for health reasons. When he was unable to go to Mass, I would bring him communion. He always looked forward to that, and when he received the Host, he would spend a few moments admiring the physical presence of his Lord and God.

Mike decided to go home during the summer. He said he thought it would help him get better. He was dying, and he knew it, but we didn't. His brother Chris and me would get his groceries for him. He was always deeply appreciative. His last words to me were, "Dad I love you!"

On the afternoon of Tuesday October 19, 2010, Michael called Chris to come over to his apartment and help him clean up a spill—not to hurry, but to bring his key to the apartment. At about 4:30, Chris found Michael kneeling in front of his chair, dead.

Obituary

Michael went to his eternal rest on Tuesday, October 19, 2010. He was born on January 9, 1962 to Mary Lou and George Phillips. He is survived by his parents; three brothers and two sisters-in-law, Robert and Kathy, George and Diana, and Christopher; three nephews and three nieces; many aunts and uncles; and best friends Julie McWright, Jim Flint, and Vinnie Palmarie.

He graduated from Seton Catholic High School and Binghamton University. He worked at Covenant House in New York City for two years. On returning home, he became a case worker at the Salavation Army in Binghamton. Michael was a CASAC drug abuse counselor for Broome County Mental Health Forensic Unit before retiring in 2008. He was honored as Counselor of the Year in 2002.

Michal was a daily communicant at St Mary's and a major contributor to Catholic Relief Services. He touched many lives as he offered his absolute respect and unconditional love to everyone he met. He would always comment that it was a pleasure to get to know someone. He will be deeply missed.

A funeral service will be held at 10:30 a.m. at Allen Funeral Home on Saturday October 23, 2010, to be followed by a Mass of the Resurrection at 11:00 at the Church of the Holy Family. Calling hours will be at Allen Funeral Home, 511 East Main Street, Endicott, on Friday October 22, 2010, from 4 to 7 p.m. In lieu of flowers, donations may made to Catholic Relief Services, PO Box 17152, Baltimore, MD 21298-8452, in Michael's memory.

Eulogy

On behalf of Michael's family I would like to thank each and everyne of you for the kindness you have extended to us in this time of pain and sorrow. The day Michael was born was one of the happiest days of my life. When the nurse came out and showed that little 5 pound 10 ounce bundle of joy I was estacic. This past Tuesday was one of the saddest days of my life when I received that phone call from his brother Chris that Mike was dead. I rush over to see Michael kneeling motionless in a prayerful position.

In the natural order of life, the parents usually predecease their children. When the child dies first we often ask why and struggle to understand God's rational. There is a story that might help us understand more, it is about a shepherd that was tending a flock of sheep in a pasture. The sheep had grazed a long time in that particular pasture. There was a pasture on the other side of the river that was much greener. The shepherd tried many times to lead his sheep over the bridge to the new pasture. But they wouldn't follow him. So he finally picked up one of baby sheep and carried it over the bridge and set it in the new pasture. When the mother sheep saw her offspring on the other side she immediate lead the other sheep over the bridge. Sometimes God uses our young to lead us to his heavenly kingdom.

The gospel we selected for Michael funeral mass was a scene from the last judgement. Jesus said when I was hungry you fed me, when I was thirsty you gave me to drink, when I was naked you clothed me, when I was ill you cared for me, when I was a stranger you welcomed me, when I was in prision you visited me. Whenever you did this to the least of my brothers you did it for me. Come you are blessed by my Father.

I couldn't imagine using any other gospel. This was Michael, it summed up his approach to life. Michael worked as a substance abuse counselor for the last twenty years. After paying his living expenses, which were very meager, he donated the rest of his income to Catholic Relief Services to feed the poor. When he was forced to retire with poor health, he wrote Catholic Relief Services that he could no longer contribute to their cause. They wrote back and thanked him for his previous support and inform him that he was their longest large-gift contributor.

When Michael graduated from high school, he spent two years in the Francisian seminary in Holyoke Mass. After spending a year at home, he returned to the Francisian community at Covenant House in New York City working with homeless kids. On his first visit home from Covenant home, he told me he had found his nitch in life working with these young people in need. He said he didn't have the training and skills he need to care for them but what he could do is love them and that is what he did.

Michael eventually learned those skills when he returned home and continued his education at Binghamton University while working as a case worker at the Salavation Army. For the past twenty years Michael was a drug and alcohol counselor for Boome County. When he was honored as the Counselor of the Year in 2002, he said at the ceremony that he could only accept the award on behalf of his fellow workers who he felt made it possible.

Michael was easy to recognize when he was walking with the black cross on the back of his clothing. The guards at the prison he worked use to call him "Big Mike". Michael wore his faith on his back as his frail body shared in the suffering of Jesus. Michael prayed constantly and he prayed daily for all his friends and relatives.

Michael was my spiritual director, he was my mentor. We walked alot together and shared alot. In fact, when I retired from IBM in the early nineties we use to walk every Sunday from downtown Binghamton to Endwell which is about seven mile. The same distant that Jesus traveled on the road to Emmaus as he share with the two disciples the meaning of his ministry. It was at a time when I was discerning my call to the diaconate ministry. Michael encouraged me to be open to God's will in my life. I look back at the joy I have experience in serving God's people these past fifteen years.

Michael had a very deep spirituality. He suffered almost constantly from his eating disorder. On one of his many visits to the doctor, his doctor shared with him that he treated many patients that had eating disorders and that they were usually quite unhappy and wondered why Michael always seemed to be so much at peace. Michael told him that everyday when he woke up he spent an hour and a half with Jesus before he left his house.

The 1st reading was from the book of Wisdom and it was at a time when most people did not believe in the resurrection from the dead. But we are a people of hope and believe that we do not die but are transformed into a new life.

And our second reading from the Book of Relevation describes this new life in that there will be a new heaven and a new earth and a holy city come down from the heavens that God will dwell in. In this new dwelling every tear will be wiped away and there will be no more pain or suffering.

The Catholic burial mass sums up our faith in Christ. As Michael body entered the church, has casket was sprinkled with holy water as a reminder of his Baptism. As the casket approached the altar the crucifix was a reminder of the need to suffer but not without hope as the casket was placed in front of the Paschal Candle a sign of the resurrected Christ. We mourn the loss of Michael but we need to rejoice and to celebrate the peace and the comfort he has finally achieved.

As a final word, Michael was in the first graduating class from Seton Catholic Central High School that started together as freshmen. Their nickname was the Saints. We thought about it last night and thought it might be nice to include "When the Saints go Marching In" in our song selection. But it was too late to make the change. I would try to sing it for you but I am afraid it would clear out the church. Oh when the saints go marching in, oh when the saints go marching in, I want to be there in that number when the saints go marching in.

.

From the *Catholic Sun,* Tuesday, January 25, 2011.

His Life is a Lesson

By Jennika Baines, Sun Associate Editor

He lived in a one-bedroom apartment in Binghamton. He had no car, few clothes, but many friends. And when he died on Oct. 19, 2010, Michael Phillips was one of Catholic Relief Service's longest large-gift contributors.

On a social worker's salary, Phillips had slowly and steadily donated a total of approximately $250,000 to the charity.

Jim Lund, vice president for charitable giving at Catholic Relief Services (CRS), said that due to donor confidentiality he was not able to say the exact figure that Michael donated during his lifetime.

"But it was in the six figures," he said. "For a substance abuse counselor, it's a substantial amount of his income."

Michael didn't designate his donation for any particular area of CRS's work, Lund said. "He gave the money to care for, in his own words, the hungry in the world."

Michael's father, Deacon George Phillips, helped Michael with his monthly budgeting and his taxes. He said there was one year when Michael made around $34,000 and donated $17,000 to CRS. "So you take the taxes out of that and you see what he had to live on," he said.

Few who knew and loved Michael had any idea the amount of money he had donated over the years. But none were surprised. Michael was very clearly someone special.

At four or five years old, Michael asked his parents if he could stay with his newly-widowed grandmother so she wouldn't be lonely. A few years later, he talked some of his pals into volunteering to rake leaves for elderly neighbors.

As a student at Seton Catholic High School, Michael belonged to a group on the outer fringes who called themselves "The Irregulars." They were the misfits: the eccentric personalities, the new kids in school, the kids who were too shy or too round to fit in elsewhere. And Michael was always finding new friends to invite into the group.

"He was a friend to the friendless," said Chris Phillips, one of Michael's three brothers.

Julie McWright grew up next door to Michael and knew all about the Irregulars. "We all came from different places of need, and he seemed to know where we all were," she said.

"He loved being Catholic, and he lived for Jesus. He suffered without ever complaining because all he did was love Jesus more than I could ever understand," McWright said. "Through his example of love, I felt like a piece of Jesus was here on earth. That's the kind of friend I was blessed with my entire life."

She remembers Michael crying with her over high school disappointments and praying for her through illnesses of her own and in her family. The two remained close even when she married and moved to another state.

"I'll tell you right now that I was his best friend," McWright said, "but I guess some other people might probably say that, too."

One of those people is Jim Flint.

The two met in high school after Flint transferred at the start of his junior year. It was the first day of football practice. Flint didn't have cleats and had to wear high-top sneakers in his old high school's colors. "Everyone called me a big spoiled brat and pretty much knocked me flat on my back all during practice," Flint said.

"Afterward, Michael came up and introduced himself, and we became friends. We were best friends from that day for the rest of my life."

Michael helped Flint manage his temper and allowed him to be the best version of himself without placing any expectations on his friend. "When you had a bad day, the phone would ring or someone would be at the door and it would be Michael. He just had that ability to know when people needed someone," Flint said.

Flint and Michael would walk to Mass or around the neighborhood, and Michael would stop in to check on elderly or sick neighbors. He would take out their trash, walk their dogs, or check that they had been taking their medication. "In this day and age, most people don't even know their neighbors," Flint said.

When Flint was married with small children and a new house, Michael knew his friend was struggling for money. At Thanksgiving, he would come by with a card with $400 in it for Christmas presents for the children. "He would insist I take it or he said he wouldn't come by anymore," Flint said.

"He was probably the most kind and generous person I have ever met," Flint said. "I will never in my entire life meet another person like Michael Phillips again."

Michael spent two years of discernment at the Franciscan seminary in Holyoke, Massachusetts, but he found that his vocation lay elsewhere. He began working at Covenant House in New York City.

There, Michael counseled teenage girls who were pregnant, runaways, or trying to escape a life of prostitution. After two years, Michael returned home to work as a case worker for the Salvation Army in Binghamton.

He went on to earn a degree at Binghamton University and began working as an alcohol substance abuse counselor for Broome County Mental Health Forensic Unit. He worked with mentally ill and addicted people in the criminal justice system.

It was a job he told his father that he wasn't sure he could handle. "He was in with all these big tough guys, but he just had a way with them," Deacon George said. "He said, 'I just prayed that I could love them as much as Jesus loved them.'"

In 2002, Michael was honored as Counselor of the Year.

"I'd walk with him on the streets of Binghamton, and quite often some former client of his would come up and say, 'Hi, Mike, I've been clean for so many years now,'" said Michael's brother George K. Phillips. "He cared for people that no one else did."

George said he also saw how passersby would mock his brother for the cross he drew on the back of his clothing and for his frail body. From his 20s onward, Michael struggled with anorexia. At his healthiest, he weighed only around 120 pounds. At his sickest, his weight would plummet closer to 80 pounds. He was in and out of hospitals and treatment centers.

But the mockery of others and the illness he struggled with only served to deepen Michael's faith. He lived in an apartment that cost him about $200 a month in rent. The furnishings were sparse, but he had a prayer bench where he would spend the first hour and a half of every day.

"He had a real relationship with Christ. He lived it daily, and it wasn't fake," his brother Chris said. "He always felt you were blessed to have faith."

Michael taught his brothers how to pray to Jesus throughout the day and even encouraged them to pray for those who had been unkind to him.

His brother Robert said Michael also had a striking ability to listen.

"He was in the present moment, and he was totally there listening and just empathizing and hearing you out," Robert said. "You'd talk to him and his sole focus would be on affirming you and making sure you were heard and understood. I think I've never had someone listen to me the way he did in my whole life."

When he was well enough, Michael would meet with his father after the noon Mass on Sunday and walk the seven miles from Binghamton to Endwell. This was at a time when Deacon George had just retired.

"Life was changing a lot for me. I didn't know what direction I was going in," he said. Michael became his father's spiritual director and encouraged him in his journey through the diaconate.

When Michael could no longer walk that distance, they would walk shorter distances. Eventually, he could only make it a few houses down the road. On Saturdays, he would walk across the street to spend some time sitting with a widow who enjoyed the company. "Some people might say he was odd, the way he didn't have new clothes or buy things," his brother George said. "He used to say did he not get it, or did the rest of us not get it? You know, 'Wait a minute, there are kids who are starving here and this is what we're doing with our money?'"

Michael moved from his parents' house back to his own apartment in the months before he died. One night in October, Deacon George had stopped by Michael's apartment to help him with his groceries. Michael was too weak to put away the boxes and bottles, so Deacon George was putting them away for him.

"When I went to leave, he looked at me and he said, 'Dad, I love you.' And it was something that he normally said, but it was the only thing he said," Deacon George said. "I think he knew."

Deacon George called Chris to say that he should check on his brother, as he didn't look good.

When Chris arrived in Michael's apartment, he found him kneeling at his prayer bench. He had died from heart failure due to his anorexia.

The night after he died, Chris and Deacon George were carrying out boxes of items from Michael's apartment to donate to Catholic Charities when a woman came up to them.

"You don't know me," she said, "but Michael changed my life."

She explained that she was a neighbor of Michael's and that she had struggled for many years with an addiction to crack cocaine. Michael would walk by her house on his way home from work and say hello to her and her daughters. After a while, he would stop and sit on the porch with them to chat. Then the chats turned to talks. One day, he brought the woman a rosary.

This, she said, was the beginning of her recovery.

The woman brought a rosary of her own that she hoped to put in Michael's casket. The one that Michael had given her, she said, she would keep with her the rest of her days.

Made in the USA
Columbia, SC
30 May 2018